Elliott Graeme, Ferdinand Hiller

Beethoven

A Memoir

Elliott Graeme, Ferdinand Hiller

Beethoven
A Memoir

ISBN/EAN: 9783742881663

Manufactured in Europe, USA, Canada, Australia, Japa

Cover: Foto ©Thomas Meinert / pixelio.de

Manufactured and distributed by brebook publishing software (www.brebook.com)

Elliott Graeme, Ferdinand Hiller

Beethoven

BEETHOVEN

A Memoir

By ELLIOTT GRAEME

WITH AN ESSAY
(*Quasi Fantasia*)
"ON THE HUNDREDTH ANNIVERSARY OF HIS BIRTH," &c.

By Dr. FERDINAND HILLER
OF COLOGNE.

"How glorious it is to live one's life a thousand times!"
BEETHOVEN.

LONDON
CHARLES GRIFFIN AND CO.
STATIONERS' HALL COURT
1870
[*The right of Translation is reserved*]

LONDON:
PRINTED BY J. AND W. RIDER,
BARTHOLOMEW CLOSE.

PREFACE.

THE following brief sketch can lay no claim to originality; it is merely a slight *résumé* of the principal events in the master's life (from the works of Schindler, Ries, and Wegeler, and more especially from Marx and Thayer), and is intended for those who, without the leisure to go deeply into the subject, yet desire to know a little more about the great tone-poet than can be gathered from the pages of a concert programme, however skilfully annotated.

The few letters introduced have been translated as nearly as possible in the manner in which they were written. Beethoven's epistolary style was simple, fervent, original, but certainly not polished.

The author feels convinced that any shortcomings in the "Memoir" will be more than atoned for by Dr. Hiller's eloquent and appreciative "*Festrede*," which seems to have been dictated by that poetic genius, the possession of which he so modestly disclaims.

E. G.

LONDON,
17*th December*, 1870.

CONTENTS.

PAGE

ESSAY *quasi* Fantasia "On the Hundredth Anniversary of Beethoven's Birth," by Dr. Ferdinand Hiller . . vii

CHAP. I.—INTRODUCTORY: Origin of the Family Van Beethoven—The Electorate of Cologne—Court of Clemens August the Magnificent—Ludwig van Beethoven the Elder—Johann van Beethoven—Bonn in 1770 1

CHAP. II.—BOYHOOD: Birth—Early Influences and Training—Neefe—First Attempts at Composition—The Boy-Organist—Max Friedrich's National Theatre—Mozart and Beethoven—Disappointment 12

CHAP. III.—YOUTH: Despondency—The Breuning Family—Literary Pursuits—Count Waldstein—National Theatre of Max Franz—King Lux and his Court—The Abbé Sterkel—Appointment as Court Pianist—First Love—Second Visit of Joseph Haydn 31

CHAP. IV.—LEHRJAHRE: Arrival in Vienna—Studies with Haydn—Timely Assistance of Schenk—Albrechtsberger—Beethoven as a Student—His Studies in Counterpoint—Letters to Eleanore v. Breuning 46

CHAP. V.—THE VIRTUOSO: Family Occurrences—Music in Vienna—Van Swieten—Prince Lichnowski—Beethoven's Independence, Personal Appearance, Manners—Rasoumowski Quartet—Occurrences in Lichnowski Palace—First Three Trios—Artistic Tour to Berlin—Woelfl—Beethoven as an Improvisatore—Steibelt 63

CONTENTS.

CHAP. VI.—CONFLICT: Deafness and its Consequences—His Brothers' Influence,—Letters to Wegeler—"Mount of Olives"—Beethoven's Will—Beethoven as a Conductor—As an Instructor—Sinfonia Eroica—"Leonora" ("Fidelio")—"Adelaide" 87

CHAP. VII.—LOVE: The Fourth Symphony—Julia Guicciardi—Letters to her—To Bettina Brentano—Beethoven's Attachments—Domestic Troubles—Frau Nanctte Streicher—Daily Life—Composing "*im Freien*" 121

CHAP. VIII.—VICTORY AND SHADOW: Period of Greatest Creative Activity—Hummel—Congress of Vienna—Maelzel—Pecuniary Difficulties—Adoption of Nephew—The Philharmonic Society—The Classical and Romantic Schools—The Jupiter Symphony—His Nephew's Conduct—Last Illness . 141

REMARKS ON THE PIANOFORTE SONATAS, BY DR. HILLER . 165

CATALOGUE OF BEETHOVEN'S WORKS 172

THE HUNDREDTH ANNIVERSARY OF BEETHOVEN'S BIRTH.*

"*Quasi Fantasia.*"

THE year 1749 brought us Goethe; 1756, Mozart; 1759, Schiller; and 1770, Beethoven. Thus, within the short space of twenty-one years four of the greatest poetic geniuses were born—four men of whom not only the German Fatherland, but all mankind must be proud.

And even more happy than proud, since the most splendid gift which the Divine Being from time to time vouchsafes to poor humanity is that of genius. Through it we receive the highest good in which we are capable of participating—the forgetfulness of self in a nobler life. Genius it is that gives us, if but for a few short hours, that which the believer awaits with earnest hope in another and a better world.

Has there ever existed a poet who transported our souls into his ideal kingdom with more irresistible force than our Beethoven? Certainly not. More universal effects have been achieved by others, but none more deep or noble. Nay, we may say without

* This Essay also appeared in Germany in the *Salon.*

exaggeration that never did an artist live whose creations were so truly *new;*—his sphere was the unforeseen.

Amidst so much that is trivial and dispiriting in art and life, the widely diffused interest, the delight in the creations of the wondrous man is a bright sign of our times. I do not say the *comprehension* of them; that is not, and cannot be the case. But there are, perhaps, no poems in the love and admiration of which so many of the highest intellects concur as the tone-poems of our master. To the essential nature of our Art, which bears within itself the all-reconciling element of love, must we attribute the fact that against it the most violent differences in religious, political, and philosophical opinion make no stand— it is the might of Beethoven's genius which subdues the proudest minds, while quickening the pulsations of the simplest hearts.

If in anything the will of man shows itself weak, nay, helpless, it is in the matter of intellectual creation. A very strong will (is not even this beyond the reach of most?) may lead to great learning, to brilliant technical acquirements, to virtue itself—a spontaneous poetic thought in word, tone, or colour, it will never be able to bring forth. Thus, the true relation of genius to us is that of a star, diffusing light and warmth, which we enjoy and admire. Since, however, to the higher man recognition and gratitude are necessities, since he desires to add intelligence and reverence to his admiration, and would willingly offer up love also to the subject of it, he begins to investigate. He asks, what the divine germ, existing even in the lisping child, demanded for its development; what brought it out into blossom—what influences worked upon it beneficially—to what extent he who was so nobly gifted was supported and furthered by moral strength—how he used the talent committed to him—finally, how he fought through the life-struggle from which no mortal is exempt.

And then he inquires again and further; which of his qualities, which of the properties peculiar to himself, affect us most strongly?—in what relation does he stand to the development of his art—in what to that of his nation?—how does he appear with regard to his own century?

A mere attempt at answering these questions, and the many connected with them, would require an enormous apparatus of a biographic and æsthetic nature, including a knowledge of the history of art and culture, and an acquaintance with musical technicalities. It does not fall either within our power or the scope of these pages to make any approach to such a task. A few slight hints may suffice to prevent our forgetting (amid the extraordinary and all-engrossing occurrences of the present time) the day which sent to us a hundred years ago the no less extraordinary man, who, a prophet in the noblest sense of the word, foresaw and declared (though only in tones) the nobleness and greatness which will be revealed by the German people, if friendly stars shine upon their future.

A species of caste seems to have been implanted

in man by nature—there are families of statesmen, warriors, theologians, artists. It will nevertheless be admitted that while it is often the case that circumstances, family traditions, cause the sons to follow in their fathers' footsteps, it frequently happens that the calling lays hold of the man, becomes, in the truest sense of the word, a *calling*.

Several of our first composers have sprung out of families in which the profession of music was chiefly followed—but certainly not many. One thing, however, was common to nearly all—they were marvellous children, prodigies. *Prodigy!* now-a-days an ominous word, recalling immediately to mind industrious fathers, who force on concerts, and musical attainments which do not refresh by their maturity, but only excite astonishment at the precocity of those from whom they are exacted. The abuse of the phenomenon has brought the latter itself into a bad light. A musical hothouse plant forced into premature bloom through vanity or the thirst for money may soon become stunted; none the less, however, does the fact remain, that no intellectual gift shows or develops itself earlier than that of music. Bach, Handel, Mozart, Hummel, Rossini, Mendelssohn, Clara Schumann, Liszt, Joachim, were prodigies. Nature knows what she is about. He alone to whom this wondrous tone-language has become a second mother tongue, will be able to express himself with freedom in it; but how soon do we begin to attempt our mother tongue! And how few succeed in really learning to *speak* it!

It would be inexplicable had not our Beethoven been also a prodigy. He was one, but after such a sound, healthy sort, that those about him were more struck by the thought of his great future, than enthusiastic about his achievements at the time. The compositions which have been preserved to us from his boyish·days bear traces, even then, of the frank, honest mode of expression which remained his to the end of his career. Naturally, their contents are trifling; what has a boy of twelve years to communicate to the world, if his inner life develop itself according to nature? Borne onwards by his artistic readiness, he attained, however, at a very early age an honourable, independent position with regard to the outer world. He had barely quitted childhood when he was organist at the Elector's Court in Bonn. At a later period he occupied for several years the post of violist in the orchestra. The viola was then one of the most neglected orchestral instruments, and we must form but a slight estimate of Beethoven's achievements upon it. It was, however, invaluable for him, the future Commander of the instrumental tone-world, to have served *in the line*. In fact, every striving young composer ought, as a matter of duty, to act for at least one year as member of an orchestra, were it only at the great drum. It is the surest method of making the individuality of the different sound organs ineffaceably one's own. When the latter are entrusted to capable executants (as was the case in the Electoral orchestra), the idea of a definite personality is added to the peculiarity of the instrument, which is not at all a bad thing. How often in later years may the image of one or other of his former colleagues have presented itself vividly and helpfully to the mind of the master, as he sat meditating over a score! How often may he have heard in spirit an expressive solo performed by one of them!

The stimulus which Beethoven received from singers in those early days at Bonn did not work very deeply. His own father, indeed, was one of the Elector's vocalists, and sang both in church and on the stage. But he was a sorry fellow, who saw in his gifted son only a means of extricating himself from his gloomy pecuniary difficulties, and certainly not the man to inspire him for the wedding of Word to Tone—the noblest union ever contracted.

Even in the most magnificent of Beethoven's vocal works there exists a certain roughness; the words domineer over the melody, or the latter over the poem. That perfect union—that melting in one another of both factors—which is peculiar to Mozart and Handel is found only separately (*vereinzelt*) in him. Would a youth spent in the midst of a great song-world have led our master along other paths?

Certainly not without significance for his development was the fact, that he was born on the lovely banks of our joyous old Rhine. Do we not sometimes hear it surging like a wave of the mighty stream through the Beethoven harmonies? Do we not feel ourselves blown upon by the fresh mountain air? And do not the cordial, true-hearted melodies, which so often escape from the master, breathe the very magic of one of those enchanting evenings which we talk or dream away on the shore of the most truly *German* stream ? The taste for an open-air life (a life *im Freien*, in freeness, as the German language so nobly expresses it) remained faithful to him until the end ; and we can scarcely picture him to ourselves better than as wandering in forests and valleys, listening for the springs which sparkled within himself.

Scientific knowledge, even in its most elementary form, was hardly presented to the notice of the young musician, and if at a later period any interest in such pursuits had arisen within him, he would have been obliged to dismiss it. On the other hand, he buried himself with his whole soul in the loftiest works of poetry, that second higher world, and always came back with renewed delight upon the works of Homer, Shakspere, Goethe, and Schiller. Many and varied were the influences which they exerted upon him. They were to him "intellectual wine," as Bettina once named his music. But those are completely mistaken who expect to find, either in them or anywhere else, positive expositions or elucidations of Beethoven's compositions, as some have occasionally attempted to do, building their theory partly on utterances of the master. When the latter refers the constantly inquiring secretary, Schindler (I know not on what occasion), to Shakspere's "Tempest," it was, after all, only an answer—nothing more. The awakening of pure musical imagination is just as inexplicable as are its results. One thing alone stands firm,—that which speaks to the heart, came from the heart,—but the life-blood which pulsates at the heart of the true artist is a thousand times more richly composed than that which flows in our veins. No æsthetic physiologist will ever be able to analyze it completely. And, in life, is it only the deep thoughts, the extraordinary occurrences, which call forth all our sensations, out of which alone our happiness and our misery are formed? Is not a calm, serene autumn day enough to entrance our inmost nature? a single verse to console us? the friendly glance of a maiden to throw us into the sweetest *reverie?* What trifling influences affect the eternally rising and falling quicksilver of our hopes! And thus the smallest occasions may have been sufficient to cause vibration in a soul so highly strung as Beethoven's. Most powerfully, however, in such a genius, worked the pure creative impulse, that eternally glowing fire in the deepest recesses of his nature, with its volcanic—but, in this instance, blissful eruptions.

We know that Beethoven proceeded as a young man to Vienna, which he never afterwards left. He found there (at least in the first half of his residence) enthusiastic admirers, intelligent friends, admission to distinguished circles, and lastly, that most necessary evil—money. Nobody will grudge to the lively, good-humoured, imperial city the fame of being able to designate as her own a brilliant line of our greatest tone-poets. But then she ought not to take it amiss that we should wonder how, within her walls, at *that* time, so magnificent an artistic development as Beethoven's should ever have been accomplished. Shall we say, not *because*, but—*in spite of* her? or shall we utter the supposition that no agglomeration of men can be sufficient for genius, since it treads a way of its own, which bears no names of streets? When, however, the question comes under discussion, of the relation of a great composer to *that* public among whom his lot is cast, we cannot deny that it is easier to understand how a Handel created his oratorios in the so-called unmusical London, than how Beethoven composed his symphonies in the musical Vienna of the period. The former found himself in London in the midst of a grand public life,—grand were the powers over which he held sway, like the continually increasing throngs of listeners who streamed to his performances. When, on the other hand, we hear of the difficulty with which Beethoven, during the course of a quarter of a century, succeeded in giving about a dozen concerts in which his Titanic orchestral poems were performed *for the first time*, we become faint at heart. And I cannot do otherwise than express my conviction that, under other conditions, no inconsiderable portion of his works, which are (to use Schumann's expression) *veiled symphonies*, would have revealed their true nature. The world of the musician would hardly have been more enriched thereby, but the musical public would have benefited. For millions would have been edified, where now hundreds torment themselves (with quartets and sonatas) for the most part in vain.

Yes! these symphonies and overtures, with their

unpretending designations, are the first poems of our time, and they are *national poems* in a far truer sense than the songs of the Edda, and all connected with them, ever can or will be for us, despite the efforts of littérateurs and artists. Yes! in the soul of this Rhinelander, who every day inveighed against the town and the state in which he lived, who was zealous for the French Republic, and ready to become Kapellmeister to King Jerome—in this soul was condensed the most ideal Germania ever conceived by the noblest mind. With the poet we may exclaim, "For he was ours!"—*ours* through what he uttered—*ours* through the form in which he spoke—*ours*, for we were true to the proverb in the way we ill-treated and misunderstood him.

"Industry and love" Goethe claims for his countrymen. No artist ever exercised these qualities with regard to his art in a higher degree than did Beethoven. *She* was to him the highest good—no care, no joy of life could separate him from her. Neither riches nor honours estranged him from the ideal which he perceived and strove after so long as he breathed. He never could do enough to satisfy himself either in single works or in his whole career. He spared himself no trouble in order to work out his thoughts to the fullest maturity, to the most transparent clearness. To the smallest tone-picture he brought the fullest power. His first sketches, like the autographs of his scores, show in the plainest manner that inflexible persistency, that unwearied patience, which we presuppose in the scientific investigator, but which, in the inspired singer, fill us with astonishment and admiration. In all conflicts (and every artistic creation is a conflict) the toughest difficulty is *to persevere.*

Truth was a fundamental part of Beethoven's character. What he sang came from his deepest soul. Never did he allow himself to make concessions either to the multitude and its frivolity, or to please the vanity of executants. The courage which is bound up with this resembles the modest bravery of the citizen, but it celebrates even fewer triumphs than the latter.

Beethoven was proud, not vain. He had the consciousness of his intellectual power—he rejoiced to see it recognised—but he despised the small change of every-day applause. Suspicious and hasty, he gave his friends occasion for many complaints, but nowhere do we find a trace of any pretension to hero-worship. He stood too high to feel himself honoured by such proceedings; but, at the same time, he had too much regard for the independent manliness of others to be pleased with a homage which clashed against that.

What a fulness of the noblest, the sublimest conceptions must have lived and moved in him to admit of their crystallizing themselves into the melodies which transport us!—softness without weakness, enthusiasm without hollowness, longing without sentimentality, passion without madness. He is deep but never turgid, pleasant but never insipid, lofty but never bombastic. In the expression of love, fervent, tender, overflowing with happiness or with melancholy, but never with ignoble sensuality. He can be cordial, cheerful, joyful to extravagance, to excess—never to vulgarity. In the deepest suffering he does not lose himself—he triumphs over it. He has been called humorous—it is a question whether music, viewed in its immediateness and truth, be capable of expressing humour—yet it may be that he sometimes "smiles amid tears." With true majesty does he move in his power, in his loftiness, in the boldness of his action, which may rise to defiance—never to senseless licence. A little self-will shows itself here and there, but it suits him well, for it is not the self-will of obstinacy, but of striving. He can be pious, never hypocritical; his lofty soul rises to the Unspeakable; he falls on his knees with humility, but not with slavish fear, for he feels the divinity within. A trace of heroic freedom pervades all his creations, consequently they work in the cause of freedom. The expression, "*Im Freien*"—liberty! might serve as the inscription on a temple dedicated to his genius!

Like Nature herself, he is varied in his forms, without ever relinquishing a deep-laid, well-concerted basis; he is rich in the melodies which he produces, but never lavish; he acts in regard to them with a wise economy. In the working out of his thoughts he unites the soundest musical logic to the richest inventive boldness. Seldom only does he forget the words of Schiller,—" In what he leaves *unsaid*, I discover the master of style."

This wise economy does not forsake him either in the selection or the number of the organs which he employs. He avoids every superfluity, but the spirits of sound which he invokes must obey him. Nevertheless, not to slavish servitude does he reduce them; on the contrary, he raises them in their own estimation by that which he exacts from them. What might be urged against him, perhaps, is that he sometimes makes demands upon them to which they are not adequate, that his ideal conception goes beyond their power of execution.

He has spoken almost exclusively in the highest forms of instrumental music, and where, in one way or other, words are added to these, he has always been actuated by high motive. He sings of Love and Freedom with Goethe, of Joy with Schiller, of the heroism of Conjugal Love in "Fidelio;" in his solemn Mass he gives expression to all those feelings which force their way from man to his Maker.

Enough, enough! we would never have done, were we to say all that could be said about such a mind. Dare we now really claim his creations, which breathe the highest humanity, as specially *German?* I think this will be granted us when we add to it the consideration that our greatest poets and thinkers have, in like manner, struck root firmly in their nationality, whence they have grown up—away, beyond—into those regions from which their glance embraced but *one* nobly striving human family.

It has been often declared that we, for long, felt and recognised our national unity only through the works of our poets, artists, and philosophers; but it has never been fully recognised that it was our first tone-poets in particular, who caused the essential German character to be appreciated by other nations. There are, perhaps, no two German names which can rejoice in a popularity—widely diffused in the most dissimilar nations—equal to that of Mozart and Beethoven. And Haydn, and Weber, and Schubert, and Mendelssohn! what a propaganda have they made for the Fatherland! That they speak a *universal* language does not prevent their uttering in it the best which we possess *as Germans.*

Nevertheless, as men are constituted, it is not to be denied that what enchants does not on that account overawe them; they *esteem* the beautiful, they *respect* only force and strength, even should these work destroyingly.

Well, then! Germany has now shown what she can do in this way; she will bloom afresh, and follow out her high aims in every direction. The consideration which we could long since have claimed as a people, will then be freely accorded to the German state.

As a musician, I can wish for the nation nothing better than that it should resemble a Beethoven symphony,—full of poetry and power; indivisible, yet many-sided; rich in thought and symmetrical in form; exalted and mighty!

And for the Beethoven symphonies I could wish directors and executants like those of whom the world's history will speak when considering the nineteenth century. But History, if at all true to her task, must also preserve the name of the man who, nearly seventy years ago, created the Eroica,—an achievement in the intellectual life which may place itself boldly by the side of every battle which has left invigorating and formative traces on the destiny of mankind.

FERDINAND HILLER.

BEETHOVEN:

A Memoir.

CHAPTER I.

INTRODUCTORY.

Origin of the family VAN BEETHOVEN—*The Electorate of Cologne— Court of Clemens August the Magnificent—Ludwig van Beethoven the Elder—Johann van Beethoven—Bonn in* 1770.

TOWARDS the middle of the seventeenth century there lived in a Belgian village near Louvain a family of the name VAN BEETHOVEN. To their position in life we have no clue, unless it be that contained in the name itself (*beet*, root ; *hof*, garden), which after all only indicates that the occupation of some remote progenitor was akin to that of the "grand old gardener" from whom we all claim descent. The question, however, is immaterial.

A member of this family left his native place, and

in the year 1650 settled in Antwerp, where he married, and became the founder of a race, one of whom was destined to render the hitherto obscure name immortal.

The grandson of this Beethoven had twelve children, the third of whom, Ludwig, followed the example of his great-grandsire, and quitted the paternal roof at an early age. It has been imagined that this step was the result of family disagreements; however that may be, it is certain that after the lapse of some years Ludwig was again in friendly correspondence with his relations.

The youth bent his steps towards the home of his ancestors, where he probably had connections, and succeeded in getting an appointment for the period of three months in one of the churches of Louvain. As this was merely to fill the place of the *Phonascus* who was ill, young Beethoven found himself when the three months were over again adrift.

He was but eighteen; tolerably well educated, however; a cultivated musician, and the possessor of a good voice. With these qualities he was pretty sure of making his way, and in the following year we hear of him at Bonn, the seat of government of the splendour-loving Clemens August, Elector of Cologne.

It has been thought that he received a special summons thither, but this is, to say the least, doubtful. It is more probable that the young man, with the love of change and the confidence in his own abilities natural to his age, was drawn to Bonn by the dazzling reports that were spread far and wide of the Mæcenas then on the episcopal throne.

A few words may not be out of place here as to the nature of the independent Ecclesiastical States (and specially of Cologne), which occupy so large a space in the history of Germany prior to the French Revolution ; since the fact of the great master having been born in one of these communities had an influence on his career which would have been wanting had fate placed him in a state of more importance, politically speaking.

We in England are inclined to hold somewhat in contempt the petty German court—the "Pumpernickel" of Thackeray,—with its formality, its gossip, its countless rules of etiquette, and its aping the doings of its greater neighbours. And yet in this ridicule there is a touch of ingratitude, for how greatly are we indebted to these "Serene Transparencies," and their love of pomp and display! How many masterpieces of art owe to their fostering care their very existence! How many men eminent in science and literature have to thank them for that support and encouragement without which their works, if produced at all, must have fallen to the ground dead-born! People talk of the divine power, the inherent energy of genius, but what a loss is it for the world when that energy is consumed in the effort of keeping soul and body together! The divine power will and does manifest itself at length, but enfeebled and distorted by the struggle which might have been averted by a little timely aid.

These prince-bishops of Cologne generally belonged to some royal house, the office being in fact regarded as a convenient sinecure for younger sons. They were chosen by the Chapter, subject only to the approval of the Pope and the Emperor, as the supreme spiritual and temporal heads, the people themselves having no voice in the matter.

They ruled over a small territory of about thirty German miles in length, and in some places only two or three in breadth. Within this limited area there were several wealthy and flourishing towns; among which, strangely enough, that which gave its name to the diocese was not included, a feud of the thirteenth century between the reigning archbishop and the burghers of Cologne having resulted in the recognition of the latter as a free imperial city, and the removal of the court to Bonn, which continued to be the seat of government until the abolition of the Electorate in 1794.

Were it not that the loss of so wealthy a town as Cologne was of no small moment to the episcopal coffers, the change must have been agreeable rather than otherwise, for Bonn even in those days fairly bore the palm from Cologne as a place of residence. Here, then, for about four hundred years the little state flourished, better perhaps than we with our modern ideas as to the union of the temporal and spiritual power are willing to admit, and especially in the last fifty years of its existence was this the case.

Debarred by the limited income at their disposal from taking any prominent part in political life, cut off from ordinary domestic ties and interests, the archbishops were driven to seek compensation for these deprivations in some favourite pursuit; and to their credit be it said, not the delights of the chase or the table alone engaged their attention. The old genius of appreciation of art transferred its presence from the Arno to the Rhine, and began to exert in the Electors of Cologne an influence of great importance in the æsthetic development of Germany.

The four last Electors especially distinguished themselves, and shed a lustre on their court, by the number of talented men they drew around them, and the liberal patronage they bestowed on music and the drama. Joseph Clemens, the first of these, was himself a composer, after the usual fashion of royal dilettanti, no doubt, but a keen discerner of talent in others.

His successor, Clemens August, had passed his youth in Rome, where, although modern taste was on the decline, the imperishable monuments of art by which he was surrounded seem to have breathed something of their own spirit into him. He did a great deal towards beautifying the town of Bonn; built, besides churches and cloisters, an immense palace, the present university, and greatly enlarged the villa of Poppelsdorf, now the Natural History Museum. His household was conducted on the most magnificent scale, grand fêtes were of common occurrence, and his court was thronged by celebrities of every rank.

Especially did the reputation of the court music

stand high. The archbishop, like his predecessor, was a connoisseur, and selections from the operas of Handel and the cantatas of Sebastian Bach were performed at Bonn in a style worthy of the imperial court at Vienna.

It was to this brilliant little capital, then, that young Ludwig van Beethoven made his way in the year 1732, with a light heart and still lighter purse, and begged for an engagement as one of the court musicians, which distinction, after the customary year's probation, was formally granted him, with an annual stipend of four hundred guldens, at that time considered a very good income for so young a man.

His career seems to have been uniformly successful and honourable. Existing documents speak of him as successively simple *Musicus*, then *Dominus van Beethoven*, next as *Musicus Aulus*, and finally in the year 1761 as *Herr Kapellmeister*, when his name also figures third in a list of twenty-eight *Hommes de chambre Honoraires* in the "Court Calendar." This success is the more remarkable when we reflect that Ludwig van Beethoven the elder was no composer, and in those days the musical director in the service of a prince was expected to produce offhand, at an hour's notice, appropriate music for every family occurrence, festival or funeral; so that his appointment as kapellmeister must have created no little jealousy, especially as there were several eminent composers at court. But in truth it would have been impossible for him to find much time for composition amid the multifarious duties that devolved upon him.

In addition to the general responsibility over all pertaining to musical matters, including the oversight of the numerous singers, choristers, and instrumentalists in the Elector's service, he was expected to conduct in church, in the theatre, on private occasions at court, to examine the candidates for vacancies in the choir and orchestra, and also to take the bass part in several operas and cantatas. Truly the Herr Kapellmeister held no sinecure, if his royal master did!

Notwithstanding, he seems to have led a quiet, even-going life, able, unlike the most of his colleagues, to lay by a little sum of money, happy in the exercise of his art (alas, poor man! domestic bliss was denied him), respected and beloved by all.

Such was the grandfather of the great Beethoven. He died when the boy was but three years of age; nevertheless the old man in the scarlet robe usually worn at that time by elderly people, with his dark complexion and flashing eye, seems to have made no ordinary impression on Beethoven's childish mind. He always spoke with reverence of his grandfather, whom he doubtless regarded as the founder of the family, and the only relic that he cared to have when settled in Vienna was a portrait of the old man, which he begs his friend Wegeler in a letter to send him from Bonn.

We have hinted that Ludwig van Beethoven was not happy in his home. If every one is haunted by some skeleton, his was grim enough. Not many years after their marriage his wife Josepha had become addicted to drinking, and in fact her habits were such that it was found necessary to place her in the restraint of a convent at Cologne. Thayer attributes this failing to grief for the loss of her children, only one of whom lived to manhood ; but this trait in her character was unfortunately reproduced in her son Johann.

The latter appears to have been a man of vacillating, inert temperament, gifted with a good voice and artistic sensibility, but not capable of any sustained effort. At the age of twenty-four we find him filling the post of Tenor in the Electoral Chapel with the miserable stipend of one hundred thalers, and not distinguished in any way, unless we except his ingenuity in spelling or misspelling his own name in the petitions which he from time to time addressed to the Elector for an increase of salary. In these he calls himself *Bethoven, Betthoven, Bethof, Biethoffen*; but this instance does not warrant us in concluding that he was a man of no education whatever, for the orthography even of those who considered themselves scholars was at that time very erratic.

At the age of twenty-seven, on an income not much larger than that just mentioned, Johann van Beethoven took unto himself a wife. The entry in the register of the parish of St. Remigius runs thus :—

"Nov. 12, 1767.

"Copulavi—

"JOHANNEM VAN BEETHOVEN, filium legitimum LUDOVICI VAN BEETHOVEN et MARIÆ JOSEPHÆ POLL,

Et
MARIAM MAGDALENAM KEFERICH,
viduam LEYM, ex Ehrenbreitstein, filiam HEN-
RICI KEFERICH et ANNÆ MARIÆ WESTROFFS."

The object of his choice was a young widow, Maria Magdalena, daughter of the head cook at the castle of Ehrenbreitstein. Her first husband, Johann Leym, one of the *valets de chambre* to the Elector of Treves, had left her a widow at the age of nineteen. The fruit of this plebeian union between the tenor singer of the Electoral Chapel and the daughter of the head cook to his Grace the Archbishop of Treves was the great maestro.

What a downfall must the discovery of this fact have been to the numerous Viennese admirers of Beethoven, who for long persisted in attributing to him a noble origin, confounding the Flemish particle *van* with the aristocratic *von!* It was impossible, they thought, that Beethoven's undoubted aristocratic leanings could be compatible with so humble a parentage. Hence the absurd fable, promulgated by Fayolle and Choron, which represented him as a natural son of Frederic II., King of Prussia, which was indignantly repudiated by Beethoven himself.

In general careless of his own reputation, he could not bear that the slightest breath of slander should touch his mother; and in a letter addressed to Wegeler begged him to "make known to the world the honour of his parents, particularly of his mother." Her memory was always regarded by him with the deepest tenderness, and he was wont to speak lovingly of the "great patience she had with his waywardness."

We cannot conclude this short sketch better than by presenting the reader with Thayer's picturesque description of Bonn, as it must have appeared in the eyes of the young Beethoven.

The old town itself wore an aspect very similar to that of the present day. There were the same churches and cloisters, the same quaint flying bridge, the same ruins of Drachenfels and Godesberg towering above the same orchard-embedded villages. The Seven Hills looked quietly down on the same classic Rhine, not as yet desecrated by puffing tourist-laden steamboat or shrieking locomotive.

Gently and evenly flowed the life-current in the Elector's capital, no foreboding of nineteenth century bustle and excitement causing even a ripple on the calm surface.

"Let our imagination paint for us a fine Easter or Whitsun morning in those times, and show us the little town in its holiday adornment and bustle.

"The bells are ringing from castle tower and church steeple; the country people, in coarse but comfortable garments (the women overladen with gay colours), come in from the neighbouring villages, fill the market-places, and throng into the churches to early mass.

"The nobles and principal citizens, in ample low-hanging coats, wide vests, and knee-breeches (the whole suit composed of some bright-coloured stuff—

silk, satin, or velvet), with great white fluttering cravats, ruffles over the hands; buckles of silver, or even of gold, below the knee and on the shoes; high frizzed and powdered perruques on the head, covered with a cocked hat, if the latter be not tucked underneath the arm; a sword by the side, and generally a gold-headed cane; and, if the morning be cold, a scarlet mantle thrown over the shoulders.

"Thus attired they decorously direct their steps to the castle to kiss the hand of his Serene Highness, or drive in at the gates in ponderous equipages, surmounted by white-powdered, cocked-hatted coachman and footman.

"Their wives wear long narrow bodices with immense flowing skirts. Their shoes with very high heels, and the towering rolls over which their hair is dressed, give them an appearance of greater height than they in reality possess. They wear short sleeves, but long silk gloves cover their arms.

"The clergy of different orders and dress are attired as at the present day, with the exception of the streaming wigs. The Electoral Guard has turned out, and from time to time the thunder of the firing from the walls reaches the ear.

"On all sides strong and bright contrasts meet the eye; velvet and silk, 'purple and fine linen,' gold and silver. Such was the taste of the period; expensive and incommodious in form, but imposing, magnificent, and indicative of the distinction between the different grades of society."

Such was the Bonn of 1770.

CHAPTER II.

BOYHOOD.

Birth—Early Influences and Training—Neefe—First Attempts at Composition—The Boy Organist—Max Friedrich's National Theatre—Mozart and Beethoven—Disappointment.

ON the 17th of December, 1770, in the old house in the Bonngasse, Ludwig van Beethoven first saw the light. He was not the eldest child, Johann having about eighteen months previously lost a son who had also been christened Ludwig.

Beethoven's infant years flew by happily, the grandfather being still alive, and able to make good any deficiency in his son's miserable income; but in the year 1773 the old man was gathered to his fathers, and the little household left to face that struggle with poverty which embittered Beethoven's youth.

The father, however, was not yet the hardened, reckless man he afterwards became, and could still take pleasure in the manifest joy exhibited by his little son whenever he sat at the pianoforte and played or sang. The sound of his father's voice was sufficient to draw the child from any game, and great was his delight when Johann placed his little fingers among the keys and taught him to follow the melody of the song.

On the title-page of the three Sonatas dedicated to the Elector Maximilian Friedrich, Beethoven says, "From my fourth year music has been my favourite pursuit;" and such would seem to have been really the case.

The readiness with which the child learned was, however, unfortunate for him. No long interval had elapsed since the extraordinary performances of the young Mozarts had astonished the whole musical world, and the evil genius of Johann van Beethoven now prompted him to turn his son's talents to the same account. He resolved to make of Ludwig a prodigy, and foresaw in his precocious efforts a mine of wealth which would do away with any necessity for exertion on his part, and allow him to give full scope to what was fast becoming his dominant passion.

With this end in view he undertook the musical education of his boy, and the little amusing lessons, at first given in play, now became sad and serious earnest. Ludwig was kept at the pianoforte morning, noon, and night, till the child began positively to hate what he had formerly adored.

Still the father was relentless: Handel, Bach, Mozart, all had been great as child-musicians; and if the boy (only a baby of five years) showed signs of obstinacy or sulkiness, he must be forced into submission by cruel threats and still more cruel punishments. Many a time was the little Ludwig seen in tears, standing on a raised bench before his pianoforte, thus early serving his apprenticeship to grief.

In short, Johann was fast doing all he could to ruin the genius of his son, when, fortunately for the world, it soon became evident that if Ludwig were to do wonders as a prodigy, he would require a better teacher than his father, and the boy was accordingly handed over to one Pfeiffer, an oboist in the theatre, and probably a lodger in Johann's house.

This man seems to have been of a genial, kindly nature, though only too willing to second his landlord's views with regard to the boy; for we learn that when the two came home from the tavern far on in the night (as was too often the case) the little Ludwig would be dragged from his bed and kept at the pianoforte till daybreak! Beethoven seems, however, to have had a great regard for Pfeiffer, who was an excellent pianist, and from whom he declared he had learned more than from any one else.

On hearing many years after that he was broken down and in poverty, he sent him, through Simrock the music publisher, a sum of money.

This ruthless conduct on the part of Johann, though unjustifiable and inhuman, probably layed the foundation of the technical skill and power over the pianoforte which so greatly distinguished Beethoven. It is not positively certain that the father gained his end, and made money by exhibiting the child, though we have the testimony of the widow Karth (who as a child inhabited the same house as the Beethovens) that on one occasion the mother made a journey to Holland and Belgium—probably to some relations in Louvain,—where she received several considerable presents from noble personages before whom the wonder-child had performed. This, however, is a mere childish reminiscence, not to be depended on, though it certainly coincides with all we know of Johann's character.

The boy was also forced to learn the violin, and this he disliked infinitely more than the piano, a fact which puts to flight the pretty anecdote narrated in the "Arachnologie" of Quatremère Disjonval, who gravely states that whenever the boy began to practise —in an old ruined garret filled with broken furniture and dilapidated music-books—a spider was in the habit of leaving its hiding-place, and perching itself upon his violin till he had finished. When his mother discovered her son's little companion she killed it, whereupon this second Orpheus, filled with indignation, smashed his instrument! Beethoven himself remembered nothing about this, and used to laugh heartily at the story, saying it was far more probable that his discordant growls frightened away every living thing—down to flies and spiders.

When he was nine years old, Pfeiffer left Bonn to act as bandmaster in a Bavarian regiment, and the boy was placed under the care of Van den Eeden, the court organist. At his death, which took place not long after, Ludwig was transferred to his successor, Christian Gottlob Neefe, whose pupil he remained for several years.

This Neefe, long since forgotten, was one of the best musicians of the time, and thought worthy to be named in the same breath with Bach and Handel. He was a ready composer, and the favourite pupil of Johann Adam Hiller, Bach's successor as Cantor in the Thomasschule at Leipzig. He appears, moreover, to have been an amiable, conscientious man, and so high did his artistic reputation stand that he, although a Protestant, was tolerated as organist in the archbishop's private chapel.

How comes it, then, that with all these qualifications Beethoven would not afterwards allow that he had profited by his instructions? The question is not easily solved. Beethoven himself wrote from Vienna to his old teacher in 1793, "I thank you for the advice which you often gave me whilst striving in my divine art. If I ever become a great man you have a share in it."

Notwithstanding this tribute there was a coldness between them. It may be that master and pupil had not that entire sympathy with each other which is essential to any worthy result from the relationship.

Beethoven, as we know, was self-willed, and overflowing with an originality which, even at that early age, would not easily brook dictation. Neefe, on the other hand, from his training in the strict Leipzig school, may have been somewhat formal and narrow in his ideas, apt to view with distrust anything unusual, and, as Thayer hints, to criticise contemptuously his young pupil's efforts in composition. If the latter conjecture be correct, it gives the clue to the earnest advice Beethoven was wont to give the critics in after years—never to judge the performances of a beginner harshly, as "many would thus be deterred from following out what they might, perhaps, have ultimately succeeded in." Contempt to a sensitive, shrinking nature is like the blast of the east wind on a tender flower; downright condemnation is easier to bear than the sneer which throws the young aspirant, smarting and humiliated, back into himself—his best energies withered for the moment.

Whatever Beethoven's feeling to Neefe may have been, it did not, at any rate, prevent his making very decided progress under his tuition, at which the organist himself rejoiced, as we learn from the following letter written by him, and published in *Cramer's Magazine*—the first printed notice of Beethoven:—"Louis van Beethoven, son of the Tenor mentioned above, a boy of eleven years, with talent of great promise. He plays the pianoforte with great execution and power, reads very well at sight, and, to say all in brief, plays almost the whole of Sebastian Bach's 'Wohl-temperirte Clavier,' which Herr Neefe has put into his hands. He who knows this collection of preludes and fugues through all the keys (which one might almost call the *non plus ultra*) will understand what this implies. Herr Neefe has also given him, so far as his other occupations permit, some introduction to the study of thorough-bass. Now he exercises him in composition, and for his encouragement has had printed in Mannheim nine variations for the pianoforte written by him on a March. This young genius deserves help in order that he may travel. He will certainly be a second Wolfgang Amadeus Mozart if he continue as he has begun."

What could be kinder than the tone of this letter?

The allusion to Mozart in the last sentence does credit to Neefe's discernment, as the great composer was at that time comparatively little known. It is to be presumed that at this period Beethoven also studied the works of C. P. E. Bach, since there is evidence that he was familiar with them. His progress, in short, was such that we find him in 1782, when he had not completed his twelfth year, installed as Neefe's representative at the organ, while the latter was absent on a journey of some duration.

Thus we may picture the boy Beethoven to ourselves, at an age when other children are frolicsome and heedless, as already a little man, earnest, grave, reserved, buried in his own thoughts, his Bach, and his organ. He had no time to join his young companions in their games, even had his inclination prompted him to do so; for besides the hours devoted to music, he attended the public school, where he went through the usual elementary course, and learned besides a little Latin. His knowledge of the latter must, however, have been very slight, as when composing his first Mass he was obliged to make use of a translation, which, considering that he was brought up in a Catholic family, is singular enough. Johann v. Beethoven was not the man to waste money, as he thought, on giving his son a liberal education, so that the degree of culture attained by Beethoven was due only to his own efforts and the influences afterwards thrown around him.

In the year 1783 the three sonatas already alluded to were published, Beethoven at the time being nearly thirteen—not *ten* years of age as was stated,—the falsifying of his age being part of his father's plan with regard to him. We give the dedication entire, because (though probably not written wholly by Beethoven himself) it offers a curious contrast to his subsequent ideas regarding the princes and great ones of the earth :—

"Most illustrious Prince! From my fourth year music has been my favourite pursuit. So early acquainted with the sweet Muse, who attuned my soul to pure harmonies, I won her, and methought was loved by her in return. I have now attained my eleventh year, and my Muse has often whispered to me in hours of inspiration, Try to write down the harmonies of thy soul! Eleven years old, thought I, how would the character of author become me? and what would riper artists say to it? I felt some trepidation. But my Muse willed it—I obeyed, and wrote.

"And dare I now, most Serene Highness, venture to lay the firstfruits of my youthful labour before your throne? and may I hope that you will cast on them the encouraging glance of your approval? Oh yes! for knowledge and art have at all times found in you a wise protector, a generous patron ; and rising talent has thriven under your fatherly care. Filled with this cheering conviction I venture to approach you with these youthful efforts.

"Accept them as the pure offering of childlike reverence, and look with favour,
"Most illustrious Prince,
"On them and their young composer,
"LUDWIG VAN BEETHOVEN."

It has been generally imagined that Neefe was paid by the Elector for the instruction given to Beethoven, but this is merely a supposition, without any proof whatever. It is more than likely that Neefe considered the assistance rendered to him by the boy an equivalent for his lessons. We have seen how, as early as 1782, he was qualified to relieve him in the organ duty, rather a heavy task, owing to the number of services at which the organist was expected to be present.

In addition to this, Neefe soon found another way of employing him—but this will require a little explanation.

Whilst awaiting his appointment as court organist, Neefe had acted as musical director to a troupe of singers known as the Grossmann Company, from the name of the directrice, Madame Grossmann. This was one of the best operatic companies in Germany, all its members being actors of experience and reputation.

Now it had entered the Elector's head to take this company into his own service, and found a national theatre (in imitation of that at Vienna) which should serve as a school of refinement for the worthy citizens of Bonn. Neefe found himself, therefore, burdened with double duties as conductor and organist, and in the season of 1783, owing to the absence of one of his colleagues (the well-known Lucchesi), was almost overwhelmed with work. He found it impossible to attend the morning rehearsals in the theatre, and accordingly young Ludwig was appointed *cembalist* in the orchestra, *i. e.*, to preside at the pianoforte. In those days this was considered a distinction (as such Haydn regarded it in London), and in fact only an accomplished musician could fill the post, as all the accompaniments were played from the score.

To this early initiation may be attributed the extreme facility with which Beethoven read, *a prima vista*, the most involved and complicated scores, even when in manuscript, and that manuscript written by a Bach in a manner calculated to drive any ordinary reader to despair.

For two years young Ludwig was the accompanist at all rehearsals, and in addition to the advantage of thus working out in the most practical way all that he learned of theory, he also gained a thorough acquaintance with the works of Grétry and Gluck.

The operas were varied by dramatic representations, and these must have had an immense influence on the observant, reflective boy; for the répertoire of the company was large, and embraced not only the standard pieces of the day, but the new plays of Lessing, and "The Robbers" of Schiller, which had begun to create a ferment of excitement throughout Germany; besides translations from Molière, Goldoni, and our own Garrick and Cumberland.

To return to our young *cembalist*, the two years 1783-84 must have been a busy time to him between the chapel and the orchestra, but not a penny did he receive for his services, although he may have earned a trifle by playing the organ every morning at the six o'clock mass in the church of St. Remigius.

When he was thirteen, however, through Neefe's influence he was nominated officially to the post he had so long filled in reality, that of assistant organist, and would have drawn a salary but for an event which threw him back again.

The Elector Max Friedrich died, the operatic company was dismissed, and Neefe, having nothing to do but play his organ, had no further need of an assistant.

This must have been a great blow to the boy; not that he cared for the money in itself, but he knew how it would have lightened his poor mother's cares, and shed a gleam of sunshine over the poverty-stricken household.

His father was now beginning to throw off all restraint; his failing was generally known, and more than once he was rescued from the hands of the police and brought home by his son in a state of unconsciousness. Long ere this, two sons, Caspar Anton Carl and Nikolaus Johann, respectively four

and six years younger than Ludwig, had been added
to the family, and doubtless many were the secret
councils between the boy and his mother as to how
the few thalers of Johann (*minus* what was spent in
the alehouse) could be made to meet the needs of the
household. It was probably about this time that
Beethoven began to give lessons, that most wearisome
of all employments to him, and so for more than a
year, to the great hindrance of his own studies, contributed his mite to the general fund.

The year 1785, however, brought with it a little
heartening; Ludwig's former appointment as assistant
organist was confirmed by the new Elector, and with
the yearly stipend of a hundred thalers an era of hope
dawned for the lad.

Max Franz, Archbishop of Cologne, was the
youngest son of Maria Theresa, and the favourite of
his brother, the Emperor Francis Joseph, whom he
strongly resembled in character and disposition.

To any one familiar with the musical history of the
period and the Emperor's relation to Mozart, this will
be sufficient to indicate the pleasure with which the
Bonn musicians must have hailed his advent. Nor
were their expectations disappointed; Max Franz
surpassed his predecessors not only in the munifi-
cence of his support, but (what is perhaps of more
importance) in the real interest shown by him in the
progress of art at his court. Neither did he confine
his patronage to music alone (though, as was natural
in a son of Maria Theresa, this was his first care);
painting, science, and literature alike felt the in-

fluence of his generous mind. The university was founded and endowed by him, and the utmost efforts made to meet that universal demand for a higher culture, and that striving after truth in art, which the works of Schlegel, Lessing, Schiller, Goethe, and others were rapidly disseminating throughout the length and breadth of Germany. As Wegeler (the friend and biographer of Beethoven, at that time a medical student of nineteen) writes, "It was a splendid, stirring time in many ways at Bonn, so long as the genial Elector, Max Franz, reigned there." It can readily be imagined, therefore, that a youth so full of promise as Beethoven could not escape the notice of such a prince, and that to his own talents, backed by the recommendation of Neefe —not to the influence of any patron—he owed the only official appointment ever held by him.

For the next year he seems to have had a comparatively easy life, his salary no doubt going to his mother, and the little he could make by teaching carefully put aside for a great purpose he had formed. A characteristic anecdote of this period is worth repeating, inasmuch as Beethoven himself used often to speak of it with glee in after life as a specimen of his boyish achievements.

In the old style of church music, on the Tuesday, Friday, and Saturday of Passion Week it was usual to sing select portions from the Lamentations of Jeremiah, consisting of short phrases of from four to six lines. In the middle of each phrase a pause was made, which the accompanist was expected to fill up as his fancy might dictate by a free interlude on the pianoforte—the organ being prohibited during these three days. Now it so happened that the singer to whom this was allotted in the Electoral Chapel was one Heller, a thoroughly well-practised but somewhat boastful musician. To him Beethoven declared that he was able to throw him out in his part without employing any means but such as were perfectly justifiable. Heller resented the insinuation, and rashly accepted a wager on the subject. When the appropriate point was reached, Beethoven ingeniously modulated to a key so remote from the original one, that although he continued to hold fast the key-note of the latter, and struck it repeatedly with his little finger, Heller was completely thrown out, and obliged abruptly to stop. Franz Ries the violinist, father of the afterwards celebrated Ferdinand, and Lucchesi, who were present, declared themselves perfectly astounded at the occurrence, and the mystified singer rushed in a tumult of rage and mortification to the Elector and complained of Beethoven. The good-humoured Max Franz, however, rather enjoyed the story, and merely ordered the young organist to content himself with a more simple accompaniment for the future.

In the spring of 1787, Ludwig at length reached the height of his boyish aspirations. His little savings had accumulated to what was in his eyes a large sum, and he looked forward with eagerness to a journey to Vienna. It has been supposed that the funds for this visit were supplied by others, but this is improbable. At that time Beethoven had no wealthy friends; there is no evidence to show that the Archbishop assisted him, and certain is it that no money was forthcoming from his father. We are obliged to fall back upon the supposition that his own scanty earnings, eked out perhaps by his mother, were his only means, especially as we know that they proved insufficient for his purpose, and that he was obliged to borrow money for his journey home.

What were Beethoven's intentions with regard to this visit?

His father's conduct, which must have many a time brought the flush of shame to his young brow, his mother's evidently failing health, the numerous unsupplied wants of the family, now increased by the birth of a daughter,—all these circumstances combined to urge on his sensitive, loving nature the necessity of making some exertion, of taking some decided step for the assistance of his dear ones.

Vienna, so far away, was his goal; there were assembled all the great and noble in art—Gluck, Haydn, Mozart! the very mention of these names must have roused the responsive throb of genius in the lad. To Vienna he would go, and surely if there were any truth in the adage that "like draws to like," these men must recognise the undeveloped powers within him, and help him to attain his object.

That some such hopes as these must have beat high in Beethoven's breast, animating him for the effort, is evident from the reaction that set in, the despair that took possession of him when he found himself forced by the iron course of events to abandon his project.

Arrived in the great capital he obtained an interview with Mozart, and played before him. The maestro, however, rewarded his performance with but feeble praise, looking upon it as mere parade; and probably in technical adroitness the boy before him was far behind the little Hummel, at that time under his tuition; for Beethoven's style, through his constant organ-playing, was somewhat heavy and rough.

Beethoven, sensitively alive to everything, perceived Mozart's opinion, and requested a thema for an improvisation. Somewhat sceptically Mozart complied, and now the boy, roused by the doubt cast upon his abilities, extemporized with a clearness of idea and richness of embellishment that took his auditor by storm. Mozart went excitedly to the bystanders in the anteroom, saying, " Pay heed to this youth—much will one day be said about him in the world !"

The amiable Mozart did not live to see the fulfilment of his prophecy, but he appears to have taken an interest in the boy, and to have given him a few lessons.

Beethoven afterwards lamented that he had never heard Mozart play, which may perhaps be accounted for by the fact that the master was much occupied at the time with his " Don Giovanni," and also had that year to mourn the loss of his father.

The following letter fully explains the cause of

Beethoven's sudden departure from Vienna, and the apparent shipwreck of all his hopes :—

"*Autumn.* *Bonn,* 1787.

"Most worthy and dear Friend,—I can easily imagine what you must think of me—that you have well-founded reasons for not entertaining a favourable opinion of me, I cannot deny.

"But I will not excuse myself until I have explained the reasons which lead me to hope that my apologies will be accepted.

"I must tell you that with my departure from Augsburg, my cheerfulness, and with it my health, began to decline. The nearer I came to my native city, the more frequent were the letters which I received from my father, urging me to travel as quickly as possible, as my mother's health gave great cause for anxiety. I hurried onwards, therefore, as fast as I could, although myself far from well. The longing to see my dying mother once more did away with all hindrances, and helped me to overcome the greatest difficulties. My mother was indeed still alive, but in the most deplorable state; her complaint was consumption; and about seven weeks ago, after enduring much pain and suffering, she died.

"Ah! who was happier than I, so long as I could still pronounce the sweet name of mother, and heard the answer! and to whom can I now say it? To the silent images resembling her, which my fancy presents to me?

"Since I have been here, I have enjoyed but few happy hours. Throughout the whole time I have been suffering from asthma, which I have reason to fear may eventually result in consumption. To this is added melancholy, for me an evil as great as my illness itself.

"Imagine yourself now in my position, and then I may hope to receive your forgiveness for my long silence.

"With regard to your extreme kindness and friendliness in lending me three carolins in Augsburg, I must beg you still to have a little indulgence with me, as my journey cost me a great deal, and here I have not the slightest prospect of earning anything. Fate is not propitious to me here in Bonn.

"You will forgive my having written at such length about my own affairs; it was all necessary in order to excuse myself.

"I entreat you not to withdraw your valuable friendship from me; there is nothing I so much desire as to render myself worthy of it.

"I am, with all esteem,
"Your most obedient servant and friend,
"L. V. BEETHOVEN,
"*Cologne Court Organist.*

"*To* Monsieur de Schaden,
   "*Counsellor at Augsburg.*"

When years afterwards Ferdinand Ries came as a boy of fifteen to Beethoven in Vienna, and solicited his help and countenance, the master, who was much occupied at the time, told him so, adding, "Say to your father that I have not forgotten how my mother died. He will be satisfied with that." Franz Ries had, in fact, at the time of the mother's illness, lent substantial assistance to the impoverished family; and this to the heart of the son was a sure claim on his lasting gratitude.

CHAPTER III.

YOUTH.

Despondency—The Breuning Family—Literary Pursuits—Count Waldstein—National Theatre of Max Franz—King Lux and his Court—The Abbé Sterkel—Appointment as Court Pianist—First Love—Second Visit of Joseph Haydn.

HOW "flat, stale, and unprofitable" must everything in Bonn have appeared to our Beethoven after the charms of Vienna—charms real in themselves, and surrounded by the ideal nimbus of his fresh young hopes and strivings! The desolate, motherless home, his neglected orphan brothers, his drunken father, the weary round of teaching,—it was no light task for an impetuous, ardent genius to lift; but it had to be faced, and with a noble self-sacrifice he entered on the dreary path before him.

He had his reward—the very occupation which he disliked more than any other, opened up to him a friendship which secured to him more peace and happiness than he had yet known, and whose influence was potent throughout his whole life—that, namely, with the family Von Breuning.

Madame von Breuning was a widow; her husband, a state councillor and a member of one of the best families in Bonn, had perished in the attempt to rescue the Electoral Archives from a fire that had broken out in the palace, and since this calamity she had lived quietly with her brother, the canon and scholar, Abraham v. Keferich, solely engaged in the education of her children. These were four in number: three boys—Christoph, Stephan, and Lenz; and one girl—Eleanore. It appears that Beethoven (who was about four years older than Stephan) was receiving violin lessons at the same time with the latter from Franz Ries; and Stephan, struck, no doubt, with the genius of his fellow-pupil, managed to get him introduced to his mother's house in the capacity of pianoforte teacher to the little Lenz. Madame von Breuning was not slow to perceive the extraordinary gifts of her son's new acquaintance; and learning incidentally, with her woman's tact, the sad state of matters at home, opened her heart as well as her house to the motherless boy. He soon became one of the family, and used to spend the greater part of the day and often the night with his new friends.

It is impossible to over-estimate the value of this friendship to the young man. What a contrast to his own neglected home did the well-ordered house of Madame v. Breuning present! Now for the first time he was admitted to mix on equal terms with people of culture; here he first enjoyed the refining influence of female society (did any remembrance of Leonore suggest his ideal heroine?); and here also he first became acquainted with the literature of his own and other countries.

The young Breunings were all intellectual, and in the pursuit of their studies they were encouraged and assisted by their uncle, the canon. Christoph wrote very good verses, and Stephan also tried his hand at some, which were not bad. The striving of these young people would naturally lead our sensitive musician to reflect on his own defective education, and to endeavour so to rectify it as to render himself worthy of their friendship. Beethoven's love of the ancient classical writers may be traced to this period, when Christoph and Stephan were studying them in the original with their uncle, though it is not probable that he ever learned Greek. His knowledge of Homer was gained through Voss's translation, and his well-worn copy of the "Odyssey" testifies to the earnest study it had received from him. French and Italian he seems to have been acquainted with so far as he deemed it necessary; but his principal literary studies were confined to Lessing, Bürger, Wieland, and Klopstock. The last especially was his favourite, and his constant companion in the solitary rambles among the mountains which he was fond of indulging in. There, alone with the nature he venerated, the sonorous lines and rolling periods of the German Milton sank deeply into his mind, to be reproduced years after in immortal harmonies. At a later period Klopstock was replaced in Beethoven's esteem by

D

Goethe, of whose poems he was wont to say that they "exercised a great sway over him, not only by their meaning, but by their rhythm also. Their language urged him on to composition."

But of all the blissful influences which tended to make this time the happiest in his life, not one was so powerful as that of Madame von Breuning herself. To her everlasting honour be it said that she was the first of the very few individuals who ever thoroughly understood the morbid and apparently contradictory character of Beethoven; and greatly is it to the credit of the latter that he merited the love of such a woman. Not his abilities alone gave him a place in her heart; it was his true, noble, generous nature that won for him a continuance of the favours first bestowed upon the artist. Madame v. Breuning thoroughly appreciated Beethoven; he felt that she did. Hence the tacit confidence that existed betweem them—he coming to her as to a mother, and she advising him as she would have done one of her own sons. Beethoven used to say of her that she understood how to "keep the insects from the blossoms."

Even she, however, sometimes failed in one point, that, namely, of inducing him to give his lessons regularly. It has been hinted before that this was an unpalatable task to Beethoven. Wegeler describes him as going to it *ut iniquæ mentis asellus*, and this dislike grew with every succeeding year. Even his subsequent relation to his illustrious friend and pupil, the Archduke Rudolphe, was in the highest degree irksome to him; he looked upon it as a mere court service. But while in Bonn our composer was not in a position to choose his occupation. "Necessity knows no law," and the higher claims of genius were forced to submit to very sublunary considerations. Madame v. Breuning's representations would sometimes succeed so far as to induce him to go to the house of his pupil; but it was generally only to say that he "could not give his lesson at that time—he would give two the next day instead." On such occasions she would smile and say, "Ah! Beethoven is in a *raptus* again!" an expression which the composer treasured up mentally, and was fond of applying to himself in after life.

About this time also Beethoven gained another friend, Count Waldstein, a young nobleman, who was passing the probationary time previously to being admitted into the Teutonic Order, at Bonn, under the Grand-Master, Max Franz. Beethoven afterwards expressed his obligations to him in the dedication of the colossal sonata Op. 53.

He became a frequent visitor to the young organist's miserable room, which he soon enlivened by the present of a grand pianoforte, and here the friends— to outward appearance so different—doubtless passed many a happy hour, for Waldstein was an excellent musician, and an enthusiastic admirer of Beethoven's improvisations.

These were also one of the great pleasures in the Breuning circle, where Wegeler relates that Beethoven would often yield to the general request, and depict on the pianoforte the character of some well-known personage. On one occasion Franz Ries, who was present, was asked to join, which he did—probably the only instance on record of two artists improvising on different instruments at one and the same time.

We have long lost sight of Johann v. Beethoven, however, and must retrace our steps to see what has become of him. By the year 1789 he had grown so hopelessly incapable that it was proposed to send him out of Bonn on a pension of one hundred thalers, while the remaining hundred of his former salary should be spent on his children. This plan was not fully carried out, but the father's salary was by the Elector's orders paid into Ludwig's hands, and entrusted to his management; so that the young man of nineteen was the real head of the family.

The Elector Max Franz now followed the example of his predecessor, and established a national theatre. Beethoven was not this time *cembalist* to the company; he played the viol in the orchestra, whither he was often accompanied by his friend Stephan Breuning, who handled the bow creditably enough. For four years Beethoven occupied this post, and the solid advantage it was to him is shown in his subsequent orchestration.

In the autumn of the year 1791 an incident occurred which broke the monotony of the court life, and gives us an interesting side-glimpse of our young musician. The Teutonic Order, referred to before, held a grand conclave at Mergentheim, at which the Elector as Grand-Master was obliged to be present. He had passed some months there the previous year, and had probably found time hang somewhat heavy on his hands; at any rate, he resolved that his private musical and theatrical staff should attend him on this occasion.

The announcement of this determination was received with great approbation by all concerned, and Lux, the first comedian of the day, was unanimously chosen king of the expedition. His Majesty then proceeded to appoint the various officers of the household, among whom Beethoven and Bernhard Romberg (afterwards the greatest violoncellist of his time) figure as Scullions. Two ships were chartered for the occasion, and King Lux and his court floated lazily down the Rhine and the Main, between the sunny vine-clad hills where the peasants were hard at work getting in the best harvest of the year. It was a merry time, and, as Beethoven afterwards said, "a fruitful source of the most beautiful images."

We can imagine the boat gliding peacefully along under the calm moonlit sky—Beethoven sitting by himself, enjoying the unusual *dolce far niente;* his companions a little apart are chanting a favourite boat-song; the harmonious sounds rise and fall, alternating with the gentle ripple on the water—and the young maestro, pondering on his future life, tries to read his destiny in the "golden writing" of the stars. Is not some such scene the background to the Adagio in the "Sonata quasi Fantasia," dedicated to the Countess Giulietta?

At Aschaffenburg, Simrock, a leading member of the company (afterwards the celebrated music-publisher), deemed it necessary that a deputation (which included Beethoven) should pay a visit of respect to the Abbé Sterkel, one of the greatest living pianists.

They were very graciously received, and the Abbé, in compliance with the pressing request of his visitors, sat down to the pianoforte, and played for some time. Beethoven, who had never before heard the instrument touched with the same elegance, listened with the deepest attention, but refused to play when requested to do so in his turn. It has been mentioned that his style was somewhat hard and rough, and he naturally feared the contrast with Sterkel's flowing ease. In vain his companions, who, with true *esprit de corps*, were proud of their young colleague, urged him to the pianoforte, till the Abbé turning the conversation on a work of Beethoven's, lately published, hinted, with disdain either real or assumed, that he did not believe the composer could master the difficulties of it himself. (The work alluded to was a series of twenty-four variations on Righini's Theme "Vieni Amore.") This touched Beethoven's honour; he yielded without further hesitation, and not only played the published variations, but invented others infinitely more complicated as he went along, assuming the gliding, graceful style of Sterkel in such a manner as utterly to bewilder the bystanders, who overwhelmed him with applause.

It was perhaps after this display that he was promoted to a higher post in King Lux's service by the royal letters patent, and to this weighty document a great seal—stamped in pitch on the lid of a little box—was attached by threads made of unravelled rope, which gave it quite an imposing aspect. Seven years afterwards Wegeler discovered this *plaisanterie* carefully treasured among Beethoven's possessions, a proof of the enjoyment afforded him by this excursion.

At Mergentheim the sensation created by the Elector's musicians was immense. In an old newspaper exhumed by the indefatigable Thayer, the following notice of Beethoven occurs.

The writer is Carl Ludwig Junker, chaplain to Prince Hohenlohe, and himself a composer and critic of no mean reputation. After giving a general account of the whole orchestra, he goes on:—

"I have heard one of the greatest players on the pianoforte, the dear, worthy Beethoven. . . . I believe we may safely estimate the artistic greatness of this amiable man by the almost inexhaustible wealth of his ideas, the expression—peculiar to himself—with which he plays, and his great technical skill. I should be at a loss to say what quality of the great artist is still wanting to him. I have heard Vogler * play on the pianoforte often, very often, and for hours at a time, and have always admired his great execution; but Beethoven, in addition to his finished style, is more speaking, more significant, more full of expression,—in short, more for the heart; consequently as good an Adagio as an Allegro player.

* One of the greatest pianists of the time.

Even the first-rate artists of this orchestra are his admirers, and all ear when he plays. He is excessively modest, without any pretensions whatever. . . . . His playing differs so materially from the ordinary mode of touching the piano, that it appears as though he had intended to lay out a path for himself, in order to arrive at the perfection which he has now attained."

But even the pleasantest things must come to an end, and the expedition to Mergentheim was no exception to the rule. In a few weeks, Archbishop, musicians, and actors were once more at Bonn, busily engaged in preparing for Christmas.

About this time Beethoven was nominated Court pianist, an appointment due partly to his friend, Count Waldstein, partly also to the following circumstance, which gave the Elector a striking proof of his young *protégé's* abilities. A new Trio by Pleyel had been sent to Max Franz, and so great was his impatience to hear it that nothing would content him but its immediate performance, without previous rehearsal, by Beethoven, Ries, and Romberg.

To hear was to obey, and the Trio was played at sight very fairly, the performers keeping well together. It was then discovered that two bars in the pianoforte part had been omitted, and supplied by Beethoven so ingeniously that not the slightest break was perceptible!

In the same year, 1791, Beethoven wrote the music for a splendid *bal masqué*, organized by his friend Waldstein, and attended by all the nobility for miles around. It was believed for long that Waldstein was the author of the music.

Beethoven, meanwhile, continued his intimacy with the Breuning family, where from time to time another attraction offered itself in the person of Fräulein Jeannette d'Honrath, a young lady of Cologne, who occasionally paid a visit of a few weeks to her friend Eleanore.

It has been asserted by some writers that Beethoven was insensible to the charms of woman, and that love was to him a sealed book! For the refutation of this statement it is only necessary to turn to his works, which breathe a very different story to such as have ears to hear. For those who have not, let the testimony of his friend Wegeler suffice: "Beethoven was *never* without a love, and generally in the highest degree enamoured." The reason why his love was fated never to expand and ripen will be explained in its own place. Here it is sufficient to say that Beethoven, while glowing with fire and tenderness, eminently calculated to love and be loved, was throughout his whole life, and in every relation, delicacy itself; his nature shrunk instinctively from anything like impurity.

To return: Mademoiselle Jeannette, a fascinating little blonde, divided her attentions so equally between Beethoven and his friend Stephan, and sang so charmingly about her heart being *desolé* when the time for parting came, that each believed himself the favoured one, until it transpired that the " Herzchen had long since been bestowed " in its entirety on a gallant Austrian officer, whom the young lady subsequently married, and who afterwards rose to the rank of general.

There does not seem to have been any attachment between Beethoven and Leonore; she was his pupil, his sister,* but nothing more; her affections were already given to young Wegeler, whose wife she afterwards became.

So our Beethoven was left to gnaw his fingers for the loss of his pretty Jeannette, and to flutter on the outside of the crowd which hovered round fair Barbara Koch, the beauty of Bonn, daughter of a widow, proprietress of a coffee-house or tavern.

What! exclaims the reader, is this an instance of the so-called "aristocratic leanings" of Beethoven?

We must beg him in reply not to look at things through exclusively British and nineteenth century spectacles. The position of worthy Frau Koch was, if not distinguished, certainly respectable.

* The following birthday greeting, surrounded by a wreath of flowers and accompanied by a silhouette of Eleanore, was found among Beethoven's papers:—

> "Glück und langes Leben
> Wünsch' ich heute Dir,
> Aber auch daneben
> Wünsch' ich etwas mir!
> Mir in Rücksicht Deiner
> Wünsch' ich Deine Huld,
> Dir in Rücksicht meiner
> Nachsicht und Geduld!
>
> "Von Ihrer Freundin und Schülerin,
> "LORCHEN V. BREUNING.

"1790."

Lewes, in his Life of Goethe, was obliged to combat with the same prejudice in his account of the poet's student days at Leipzig, and we cannot do better than quote his words with regard to the society to be found in a German Wirthshaus of the period :—

"The *table d'hôte* is composed of a circle of habitués, varied by occasional visitors, who in time become, perhaps, members of the circle. Even with strangers conversation is freely interchanged, and in a little while friendships are formed, as natural tastes and likings assimilate, which are carried out into the current of life."

The habitués of Frau Koch's house were the professors and students at the university, and such members of the Electoral household as were engaged in artistic pursuits. It was a rendezvous for them all, where science, literature, art, and politics were discussed by able men ; and here, doubtless, Beethoven, with his friends Stephan Breuning and young Reicha (nephew of the director), spent many a pleasant evening. The fair Babette was, as we have hinted, no small attraction. She was a cultivated woman, and the great friend of Eleanore v. Breuning. She afterwards became governess to the children of the minister Count Belderbusch, whom she finally married.

We now come to an event which completely changed the current of Beethoven's life—the return of Joseph Haydn from his second visit to London. As he passed through Bonn the musicians gave him a public breakfast at Godesberg, on which occasion

Beethoven laid before him a cantata of his composition —probably that on the death of Leopold II. It met with the warmest praise from Haydn, but on account of the difficulty of the passages for wind instruments, was never printed.

Whether the arrangements were made at this time for Haydn's reception of Beethoven as his pupil, or negotiated afterwards through Waldstein, is not known. Certain it is that in the October of 1792 we find his long-delayed hopes on the point of realization, a pension from the Elector having removed all difficulties.

Beethoven had often bemoaned in secret, and specially to his friend Waldstein, the irregular, broken instruction he had received, attributing Mozart's early success to the systematic course of study he had pursued under the guidance of his father. It is a question, however, whether Beethoven—even had he enjoyed the advantages of Mozart—would ever have composed with the facility of the latter. Thayer thinks not; there is evidence enough in the symphonies, &c., of our great master to prove that he "earned his bread by the sweat of his brow."

The following note from Waldstein evinces the deep interest he took in Beethoven, and his faith in the young composer's genius:—

"DEAR BEETHOVEN,—"You are now going to Vienna for the realization of your wishes, so long frustrated. The Genius of Mozart still mourns and laments the death of his disciple. He found refuge with the inexhaustible Haydn, but no scope for action, and through him he now wishes once more to be united to some one. Receive, through unbroken industry, the spirit of Mozart from the hands of Haydn.

"Your true friend,
"WALDSTEIN.

"Bonn, 29*th October*, 1792."

In the beginning of November, then, 1792, Beethoven finally took leave of his boyhood's friends —father and brothers, Wegeler, Franz Ries, Neefe, Reicha, Waldstein, pretty Barbara Koch, and, hardest of all, the Breunings.

Some of these he saw for the last time.

He was destined never again to tread the old familiar streets of Bonn.

CHAPTER IV.

LEHRJAHRE.

Arrival in Vienna—Studies with Haydn—Timely Assistance of Schenk—Albrechtsberger—Beethoven as a Student—His Studies in Counterpoint—Letters to Eleanore v. Breuning.

BEHOLD, then, our young musician at the long-desired goal—free from all depressing, pecuniary cares, with his pension secure from the Elector, and a little fund of his own to boot. He reached the capital about the middle of November, alone and friendless; nor is there any proof that the advent of the insignificant, clumsily built provincial youth made the slightest sensation, or roused the interest of one individual among the many thousands who thronged the busy streets.

His first care, as shown from a little pocket-book still preserved, was to seek out a lodging suitable to his slender purse; his next, to procure a pianoforte. The first requirement he at length met with in a small room on "a sunk floor," which commended itself by the low rent asked for it. Here Beethoven contentedly located himself until fortune's smiles had begun to beam so brightly on him that he felt entitled to remove to more airy lodgings.

We may be sure that he lost no time in setting about the purpose which he had most at heart, and enrolling himself among Haydn's pupils, for he could not have been more than eight weeks in Vienna when the master wrote to Bonn, " I must now give up all great works to him [Beethoven], and soon cease composing."

The harmony, however, which at first existed between Haydn and his pupil was soon disturbed. The former seems to have been always pleased with the work executed by Beethoven, who, on the contrary, was very much dissatisfied with the instruction given by the master. He was obliged, in this instance, to make the same experience that he had formerly confided to Junker, at Mergentheim, regarding pianoforte players, viz., that he had seldom found what he believed himself entitled to expect. Distance lends enchantment to the view; and the keen, striving worker soon discovered that Haydn was not the profound, earnest thinker that his longing fancy had painted in Bonn.

But an unexpected help was at hand. One day as he was returning from his lesson at Haydn's house, his portfolio under his arm, he met a friend whose acquaintance he had only recently made, but with whom he was already on intimate terms—Johann Schenk, a thorough and scholarly musician, afterwards well known as the composer of the "Dorfbarbier," and one of the most amiable of men. To him Beethoven confided his troubles, bitterly lamenting the slow progress his knowledge of counterpoint made under Haydn's guidance. Somewhat astounded, Schenk examined the compositions in Beethoven's portfolio, and discovered many faults which had been passed over without correction.

Haydn's conduct in this instance has never been explained. Generally conscientious in the discharge of his duties as an instructor, this carelessness must have arisen either from a pressure of work, or from some undefined feeling with regard to Beethoven, which prompted him to give him as little assistance as possible. The latter supposition is hardly compatible with the terms in which he wrote of his pupil to Bonn, but Beethoven could never shake off the idea that Haydn did not mean well by him—a suspicion which was strengthened by what afterwards occurred.

Excessively irritated by Schenk's discovery, Beethoven would have gone on the impulse of the moment to reproach Haydn and break off all connection with him. Schenk, however, who had early perceived Beethoven's worth, succeeded in calming him, promising him all the assistance in his power, and pointing out the folly of a course which would inevitably have led to the withdrawal of the pension from Max Franz, who would naturally have disbelieved any complaint against the greatest master of the day, and have attributed Beethoven's conduct to wrong motives. The young man had the sense to perceive the justice of these remarks, and continued to bring his work to Haydn (Schenk always giving it a strict revisal) until the latter's journey to England in 1793 afforded a feasible opportunity of providing himself with a better teacher.

Thus, although neither cordially liked the other, a tolerable appearance of friendship was maintained. It was, perhaps, impossible that between two such totally different natures the connection could have been otherwise. Haydn was genial and affable; from his long contest with poverty rather obsequious, not apt to take offence or to imagine slights; ready to render unto Cæsar his due; in short—a courtier.

What greater contrast to all this can be imagined than our proud, reserved, brusque Beethoven? *He* pay court to princes, or wait with "bated breath" upon their whims! He, the stormy republican, who regarded all men as on the same level, and would bow to nothing less than the Divine in man!

Haydn, who had laughingly bestowed on him the title of the "Great Mogul," probably felt that there was no real sympathy, or possibility of such a feeling, between them. Nevertheless, as we have said, they continued to outward seeming friends, though Beethoven's suspicions would not allow him to accept Haydn's offer of taking him to London. He accompanied him, however, in the summer to Eisenstadt, the residence of Prince Esterhazy, Haydn's patron, and on this occasion left the following note for Schenk, which shows the friendly feeling existing between them:—

"Dear Schenk,—I did not know that I should set off to-day for Eisenstadt. I should like much to have spoken once more to you. Meanwhile, depend upon my gratitude for the kindnesses you have shown me. I shall endeavour, so far as is in my power, to requite you.

"I hope to see you soon again, and to enjoy the pleasure of your society. Farewell, and don't quite forget

"Your Beethoven."

One of Beethoven's peculiarities may as well be referred to here in passing. Although living in the same town with many of his friends—nay, within a few minutes walk of them,—years would elapse without their coming in contact, unless they continually presented themselves to his notice, and so *would* not let themselves be forgotten. Absorbed in his creations, the master lived in a world of his own; consequently, many little circumstances in his career, in reality proceeding from this abstraction, were at the time attributed to very different motives.

His connection with Schenk is an instance of this. Though both inhabited Vienna, they had not met for many years, when in 1824 Beethoven and his friend Schindler encountered Schenk—then almost seventy years of age—in the street. If his old teacher had spent the intervening years in another world, and suddenly alighted from the clouds, Beethoven could not have been more surprised and delighted. To drag him into the quietest corner of the "Jägerhorn" (a tavern close at hand) was the work of a moment, and there for hours the old friends mutually compared notes, and reviewed the ups and downs of fortune that had befallen them since the days when the Great Mogul used to storm Schenk's lodgings and abuse his master. When they parted it was in tears, never to meet again.

The opportune departure of Haydn allowed Beethoven to place himself under the instruction of Albrechtsberger, the cathedral organist. This man, who counted among his pupils not only Beethoven, but Hummel and Seyfried, was a walking treatise on counterpoint; but far from investing the science with any life or brightness, it was his delight to render it, if possible, more austere and stringent than he had found it, and to lay down rules which to a fiery, impulsive nature were positively unbearable. Nevertheless, Pegasus can go in harness if need be. Beethoven, who, like every true genius, was essentially modest in his estimate of himself, and had already felt the want of a thoroughly grounded knowledge, submitted to Albrechtsberger's routine for a period of about eighteen months—beginning almost at the elements of the science, and working out the dry-as-dust themes in his master's Gradus ad Parnassum, until he had solved for himself the mysteries of fugue and canon.

This is not the commonly received notion of Beethoven's student-days. Ries in his "Notices" has the following :—

"I knew them all well [*i. e.*, Haydn, Albrechtsberger, and Salieri, who gave Beethoven instruction in writing for the voice]; all three appreciated Beethoven highly, but were all of *one* opinion regarding his studies. Each said Beethoven was always so obstinate and self-willed that he had afterwards much to learn through his own hard experience, which he would not accept in earlier days as the subject of instruction. Albrechtsberger and Salieri especially were of this opinion."

But this testimony ought not to be accepted for more than it is worth. Haydn, absorbed in his own pursuits, and utterly unable to fathom Beethoven's nature—the very reverse of his own; Albrechtsberger, the formal contrapuntist, far more concerned about the outside of the cup, the form of a composition, than about its contents; Salieri, the superficial composer of a few trashy operas long since forgotten,—how were these men competent to pass judgment on a *Feuerkopf* like Beethoven?

A few extracts,* taken at random from the marginal notes scribbled on the books in which Beethoven's exercises in composition were written (published after his death by the Chevalier von Seyfried), will enable the reader to judge whether the master was an earnest, willing student or no :—

"Continual dropping wears out a stone, not by force, but by constant attrition. Knowledge can only be acquired by constant diligence; we may well say, *nulle dies sine lineâ*—no day without its line;

---

* From Beethoven's "Studies in Thorough-bass," published by the Chevalier v. Seyfried, and translated by Henry Hugh Pierson.

every day that we spend without learning something is a day lost. Man possesses nothing so costly and precious as time; therefore let us not postpone till to-morrow what may be done to-day."

Tempora mutantur!—How will a future age regard and criticise the most admired works of our favourite composers! Seeing that almost everything is subject to change, and, alas! to the caprices of fashion, it is clear that only works of sterling value and intrinsic excellence can survive; these alone can bid defiance to mutability and false taste. Therefore let the composer, the poet of Sound, disregard the passing mode, and cling resolutely to the imperishable laws of the Beautiful. True Art is neither the slave of fashion nor of pedantry; it soars triumphantly above both! Let us also never forget that no genius can make up for superficial learning or want of diligence. The artist's motto is:—Persevere! Life is short—art is long!"

"While we acknowledge that the old masters were fully justified in adhering to simplicity, we cannot desire to imitate them in their blind obedience to arbitrary laws, some of which are mere millstones round the neck of imagination, only serving to frighten the beginner and impede his progress. Time goes on, and what sufficed for one age appears to the next a woeful shortcoming. Let me not be supposed to advocate an impertinent contempt of the great principles of art, *which are unchangeable;* I would only say that as time advances, art also advances in many things. Invention and fancy must not be denied the rights and privileges of which schoolmen, theorists, and barren critics would gladly deprive them. . . . And yet I would advise a composer rather to be commonplace than far-fetched in his ideas, or bombastic in his expression of them."

"I determined for once to avail myself of the old axiom, '*Nulla regula sine exceptione*,' and therefore began with a sixth, *i.e.*, wrote an imperfect chord in the first bar, where, *ex officio*, a perfect chord should stand. But I solemnly pledge myself not to commit this mortal sin again (though I can't say that I repent of it!) and in making a four-part composition of it will not fail to write the third, *A*, under the tenor, *C*, which will produce a complete quadricinium; then I shall have appeased the angry gods, I mean the learned Thebans or pedants, who must then, *nolens volens*, acquit me!"

"Many theorists are of opinion that every piece in a minor mode ought properly to conclude in the same. *Nego!* On the contrary, I think the major third taken as the close has a much finer effect, and is very soothing to the ear and mind; joy comes after grief, sunshine after storm. The close with the major third gives me the same tranquillizing feelings as when I gaze upon the soft light of the evening star."

"I would beg, parenthetically, to observe that I have had the temerity to introduce a dissonant interval here and there, sometimes leaving it abruptly, sometimes striking it without preparation. I hope this is no high treason, and that the *judices doctissimi*, if I ever meet them in the Elysian fields, will not shake their periwigs at me. I did this to preserve the vocal melody intact, and will be responsible for it before any tribunal of common sense and good taste. Passages that are easy to sing, and are not far-fetched or difficult to hit, cannot be faulty. These severe laws were only imposed upon us to hinder us from writing what the human voice cannot execute; he who takes care not to do this need not fear to shake off such fetters, or at least to make them less galling. Too great caution is much the same as timidity. *Satis pro peccatis:* here is a long defence of a slight misdemeanour!"

"An antiquated rule makes it unlawful to go beyond the six nearest relative keys in a strictly conducted fugue; but I am decidedly of opinion that one need not scruple to infringe this rule; if a man have sharp eyes, and can walk well, he may venture to go a little beyond the prescribed limits without danger."

At the end of the notes on simple counterpoint, he writes :—

"*Omnia ad majorem Dei gloriam!* Patience, diligence, perseverance, and a steady determination, carry one to the goal."

The sarcastic tone of some of these remarks is indicative of Beethoven's inflexible determination to shake off all restraints, the utility of which were not recognised by his inner consciousness. Ries relates that on one occasion he pointed out to him in one of his earlier quartettes two perfect fifths in succession.

"What does that signify?" asked the master, testily.

"But it *must* be wrong," pursued the scholar, astounded.

"Who says so?"

"Kirnberger, Fuchs, Marpurg—all the theorists."

"Let them say it!" was the rejoinder; *i.e.*, 'I maintain it is *not* wrong.'

In after years, when told of any perplexity of the critics, he would rub his hands together in glee, saying, "Yes, yes; they are all astonished and put their heads together because they don't find it in any Thorough-bass book."

On one occasion a friend had remarked, regarding the second and third "Leonora" overtures, "The artist must create in freedom, only giving in to the spirit of his age, and be monarch over his own materials; under such conditions alone will true art-works come to light."

"Granted," replied Beethoven; "but he must *not* give in to the spirit of his age; otherwise it is all over with originality. . . . Had I written them [the two overtures] in the spirit that prevailed at the time, they would certainly have been understood at once, as, for example, the Storm of Kotzeluch. But I cannot cut and carve out my works according to the fashion, as they would fain have me do. Freshness and originality create themselves, without thinking about it."

But while thus probing and contesting all the received theoretical axioms, while Albrechtsberger's hair stood on end at his daring innovations, Beethoven was most indefatigable in his practical investigations into the nature and capabilities of the instruments for which he wrote, and which his creative genius roused to unheard-of achievements. From Herren Kraft and Linke he learned the mechanism of the violoncello; Punto taught him that of the horn, and Friedlowsky that of the clarionet. He often consulted these artists in after life regarding the suitability of certain passages for their respective instruments, and allowed himself to be guided by their suggestions.

Far otherwise was it, however, with singers; for them Beethoven composed as he liked, without humouring any little predilection of the most fascinating prima donna, or introducing a single piece for display (one reason why Rossini was able for so long to play the part of the successful rival). On the other hand, the singers had their revenge, and sang his music precisely as they listed, interpolating embellishments and cadenze *a piacere* without the slightest regard to his wishes.

The following letters to Eleanore van Breuning belong to this epoch:—

"*Vienna, Nov. 2nd,* '93.

"MOST ESTEEMED ELEANORE! MY DEAREST FRIEND!—A whole year of my residence in the capital has nearly elapsed without your having received a letter from me, notwithstanding you have been continually with me in the liveliest remembrance. I have often entertained myself with the thought of you and your dear family, but oftener still I have not enjoyed the peace in doing so which I could have wished.*

"At such times that fatal dispute hovered before me, and my conduct in the matter appeared to me detestable. But it was past and gone. How much would I give to be able to obliterate entirely from my life the way in which I then acted! so dishonouring to me, so opposed to my general character. At the same time there were many circumstances which tended to keep us apart, and I suspect that what specially hindered a reconciliation was the manner in which the remarks of each were repeated to the other. We both believed that what we said was the result of honest conviction, when in reality it proceeded from anger inflamed by others, and so we were both deceived. Your good and noble character, my dear friend, warrants me in believing that you have long since forgiven me; but they say that the truest repentance is that in which we confess our own faults, and this is what I desire to do. And let us now draw the curtain over the whole affair, only extracting the lesson from it that when a dispute happens between friends, it is always better that no mediator should be employed, but that friend should address himself direct to friend.

* The following remarks are eminently characteristic of Beethoven. When his fiery nature had led him into saying or doing anything which subsequent reflection showed him to be contrary to true friendship, his remorse knew no bounds. Wegeler declares that his contrition was often entirely disproportionate to the fault committed, as in the present instance.

"You will receive along with this a dedication,* and I can only wish that it were greater and more worthy of you. They teased me here into publishing this little work, and I avail myself of the opportunity to give you, my esteemed Eleanore, a proof of my regard and friendship for yourself, and a token of my lasting remembrance of your house. Accept this trifle, and think of it as coming from a devoted friend. Oh! if it only gives you pleasure, my wishes will be quite satisfied. May it be a little reawakening of the time when I passed so many happy hours in your house! perhaps it may keep you in remembrance of me until I return again, which certainly will not happen soon. Oh! my dear friend, how we shall rejoice then! You will find your friend a more cheerful man, with all the former furrows of adversity chased away through time and a happier lot.

"If you should see B. Koch, I beg you to tell her that it is unkind of her not to have written me even once. I have written to her twice, and to Malchus † three times—but no answer. Tell her that if she will not write herself, she might, at least, urge Malchus to do so.

"In concluding my letter, I venture one more request, namely, that it would make me very happy to possess an Angola vest knitted by your hands, my dear friend. Forgive this not very modest demand!

---

* Variations on Figaro's air, "Se vuol ballare."
† Afterwards Count Marienrode, and Minister of Finance in the kingdom of Westphalia. At a later period he filled the same office in Wirtemberg.

It arises out of my great predilection for everything made by you; but I must tell you confidentially that there is also a little vanity connected with it. I want to be able to say that I possess something of one of the best and most admired girls in Bonn. I have, it is true, still the first which you kindly gave me in Bonn, but it has become so old-fashioned that I can only treasure it up in my wardrobe as something of yours, very dear to me. You would delight me much by favouring me soon with one of your kind letters. Should mine give you any pleasure, I promise you certainly, so far as lies in my power, to continue them; since everything is welcome to me whereby I may prove to you how much I am,

"With all esteem,
"Your true Friend,
"L. V. BEETHOVEN.

"P.S.—You will find the v. [variations] somewhat difficult to play, especially the shake in the coda; but don't let this alarm you, since it is so arranged that you have nothing to do but the shake; the other notes you may leave out, as they occur in the violin part. I would never have written in this manner had I not had occasion to remark that there are several people here in V., who, after I have extemporized of an evening, write down many of my peculiarities next day, and pass them off as their own.* As I

---

* Wegeler says, "Beethoven often complained to me also of this sort of *espionage*. He particularized the Abbé Gelinek, a very fruitful composer of variations, in Vienna, who always settled himself in his

foresaw that such things would soon be published, it occurred to me to anticipate their movements. Another reason was also—to perplex the pianoforte teachers here. Many of them are my mortal enemies, and I wished to revenge myself on them in this way; knowing that they would occasionally be asked to play the variations, when these gentlemen would come out in rather an unfavourable light."

The following fragment is without date :—

"The beautiful cravat, worked by your own hands, has caused me the greatest possible surprise. Although in itself so pleasing, it awakened within me feelings of melancholy. Its effect was to recall the past, and to shame me by your generous behaviour. In truth, I did not think that you still considered me worthy of remembrance.

"Oh! could you have been a witness of my emotions yesterday when it arrived, you would not think I exaggerate in saying that the recollection of you brings the tears to my eyes, and makes me very sad. However little I may deserve credit in your eyes, I beg you to believe, *my friend* (allow me still to call you so), that I have suffered and still suffer through the loss of your friendship. You and your dear mother I shall never forget. Your goodness to me was such that the loss of you neither can nor will be easily replaced. I know what I lost and what you were to me, but——if I attempt to fill up this blank,

---

neighbourhood. This may have been one of the reasons why Beethoven always looked out for a lodging in as open a place as possible."

I must refer to scenes which are as unpleasant for you to hear as for me to describe.

"As a slight return for your kind remembrance of me, I take the liberty of sending you some variations, and the rondo with violin accompaniment. I have a great deal to do, or I would have copied the long-promised sonata for you. In my manuscript it is little better than a sketch, and it would be very difficult for Paraquin himself,* clever as he is, to transcribe it. You can have the rondo copied, and then return the score to me. It is the only one of all my compositions suitable for you, and as you are shortly going to Kerpen,† I thought it might afford you some pleasure.

"Farewell, my friend. It is impossible for me to call you by any other name, however indifferent I may be to you. Pray believe that I reverence you and your mother as highly as formerly.

"If it is in my power to contribute anything to your happiness, pray do not fail to let me know, since it is the only means left to me of proving my gratitude for past friendship.

"May you have a pleasant journey, and bring your dear mother back in perfect health!

"Think sometimes of

"Your admiring Friend,

"BEETHOVEN."

---

* *Paraquin*, contro-basso in the electoral orchestra; a thorough musician, and universally esteemed as such.

† *Kerpen*, the residence of an uncle of Fraulein v. Breuning, where the family usually spent some weeks in summer.

CHAPTER V.

THE VIRTUOSO.

Family Occurrences—Music in Vienna—Van Swieten—Prince Lichnowski—Beethoven's Independence, Personal Appearance, Manners—Rasumowski Quartet—Occurrences in Lichnowski's Palace—First Three Trios—Artistic Tour to Berlin—Woelfl—Beethoven as an Improvisatore - Steibelt.

BEETHOVEN'S period of study embraced nearly three years, during which many events took place that produced a revolution in his circumstances, and left him at their close in a very different position from that in which they had found him.

The first of these was the death of his father, which happened about a month after his arrival in Vienna, obliged the young man to take upon himself once more the duties of guardian to his two brothers, and necessitated the following petition to the Elector:—

"MOST REVEREND AND GRACIOUS PRINCE,—Some years ago your Highness was pleased to grant a pension to my father, the court tenor Van Beethoven, and graciously to decree that one hundred thalers of his salary should be placed in my hands, that I might provide for the clothing, maintenance, and education of my two younger brothers, and also discharge the debts contracted by our father. I wished at once to present this order to your Highness's treasurer; but my father earnestly implored me not to do so, that it might not be imagined he was incapable of superintending his own family; and he further added that he would himself pay me quarterly the twenty-five R. thalers, which up to the present time was faithfully performed.

"After his death, however (in December last), when I wished to avail myself of your Highness's kindness and present the above-mentioned order, I was alarmed by the discovery that my father had made away with it.

"With all dutiful respect I therefore beg your Serene Highness kindly to renew this order, and to instruct your treasurer to let me have the last quarter of this gracious addition to my salary (due the beginning of February).

"Your Serene Highness's
"Most obedient and faithful Servant,
"LUD. V. BEETHOVEN, *Court Organist.*"

This request was granted, and Franz Ries undertook the management of the money; but after June, 1793, not only this but the pension granted to Beethoven himself was suddenly stopped. The fruits of the French Revolution had made themselves apparent, and the Elector was forced to fly from Bonn and take refuge in Mergentheim. Henceforth, Beethoven must depend upon himself.

Luckily the emergency found him prepared ; he was already esteemed as one of the best pianoforte players of the day—nay, there were not wanting those who assigned to him the very first place. The recommendation of Count Waldstein, who was nearly related to more than half a dozen of the best families in Austria, coupled with that of the elector (uncle to the reigning emperor), together with the fact that he was Haydn's most promising pupil, gained for the young man admission to the highest circles in the capital, where his extraordinary abilities speedily met with recognition, and placed him above all fear of want.

In accounting for the peculiar facility with which Beethoven obtained a hearing in Vienna, the state of society and position of art at the period must not be forgotten.

In a wide sense, and as we should understand it now, music was not universally cultivated or appreciated. The opera houses were two in number, one entirely given up to Italian performances ; the other plain and unattractive, struggling under great disadvantages to bring forward native composers.

Church music was at a low ebb ; the influence of Albrechtsberger at the cathedral not tending to much life or novelty in that branch of composition.

Public concerts, such as are now of daily occurrence, happened perhaps once a year, when funds were required for some charity.

Thus, music was not then the universal pursuit of all classes. The enjoyment of it was almost entirely limited to the privileged few—the aristocracy—who, following the example set by the reigning family, professed an adoration of the art, a devotion to it, which (though, of course, in many instances genuine) was so general, so common, as to cast a doubt upon its reality. Music was, in short, the fashionable rage; to be non-musical was to shut oneself out of the pale of society—an alternative not to be thought of without shuddering by the gay, pleasure-loving Viennese.

Accordingly the musical enthusiasm was wonderful. We find no less than ten private theatres, each with its full corps of actors and actresses, at most of which operettas were performed; and an orchestral society, composed exclusively of members of noble houses, who gave public concerts, open only to their equals in society, at the unwonted hour of six in the morning.

In addition to these, every nobleman had his private orchestra, or his *Quartettistes*, or, if his means would not admit of this, at least one eminent instrumental player, attached to his household. As all the great families of Austria vied with each other in the splendour and *recherché* style of their musical entertainments, it may easily be imagined how, in such a state of society, Beethoven was lionized, petted, and fêted.

Thayer gives a list of no fewer than thirty-one great houses (nine of them belonging to princes) which must have been open to him, as the owners were all recognised, worthy dilettanti in the highest sense—not mere followers of the fickle goddess, Fashion. Add to these the crowd that is ever ready to patronize him whom the leaders of *ton* have taken by the hand, and we see that Beethoven could not have wanted either for pupils or for opportunities of playing at private concerts.

It was, doubtless, the bustle and pressure of this episode in his life, the contact with vulgarity in high places, that gave him the dislike he afterwards manifested to playing in public. At an earlier period in Bonn, as we have seen, it was his delight to communicate his ideas to others, and to pour forth the inmost feelings of his soul in the presence of a little circle of sympathising, cultivated listeners. But here, in Vienna, to play at the command of some birth-proud aristocrat, who regarded art and artists as mere ministers to his pleasure—from such a task Beethoven's mind revolted. Wegeler relates the effect which such an occurrence would have upon him :—

" An invitation to play in society robbed him of all gaiety. He would come to me gloomy and downcast, complaining that he was forced to play till the blood tingled to his very finger tips. By degrees we would begin to talk together in a friendly way, when I sought to distract his thoughts and to soothe him. When this end was achieved, I let the conversation drop. I placed myself at my desk, and if Beethoven wished to speak to me again, he was obliged to seat himself on a chair before the pianoforte. Soon, and often without turning, he would strike a few undecided chords, out of which the most beautiful melodies were gradually developed. I dared not hazard a remark about his playing, or only allude to it *en passant*. Beethoven would go away quite cheerful, and always return willingly to me. The dislike, however, remained, and was often the occasion of a rupture between him and his best friends."

But the halcyon days had not yet arrived when the great tone-poet could devote himself entirely to his life-mission. His own wants and those of his brothers had to be provided for, and accordingly the round of pianoforte-playing was gone through, as that of teaching had been before, and with the same result, it paved the way to life-friendships.

Amongst the distinct leaders of the musical taste of the capital was Gottfried, Baron van Swieten, the son of Maria Theresa's Dutch physician, and the composer of twelve symphonies (on which Haydn's verdict was—"as stiff as himself.") He had formerly passed some time in Berlin, where he had become acquainted with Friedemann and Emanuel Bach, and had heard the "Messiah," "Judas Maccabæus," and "Alexander's Feast." After his return to Vienna, he acted as secretary to a musical society which met at his house, where the great works of Bach, Handel, and the old Italian writers (including Palestrina), were devotedly studied. Mozart's co-operation in this undertaking had been invaluable; but Mozart was gone, and Van Swieten was inconsolable for his loss until he discovered Beethoven. He was a quaint type of a race long extinct—the genuine old *kenner* or connoisseur. One can almost see him, when at a concert an incautious whisper was heard in the background, rising majestically from his place, and conspicuous from his great height, taking an awful survey of the room to discover the offender and wither him by a glance! In his efforts after the *true* in art, however, no very marked line was discernible to him between the sublime and the ridiculous; hence the earnestness with which he persuaded Haydn (and for which the latter never forgave him) to insert the croaking of the frogs in the Seasons. But take him for all in all, he was a valuable friend to Beethoven, and as such the latter regarded him. A carefully preserved note of his is still extant: "If nothing comes in the way, I should like to see you here next Wednesday, at half-past eight o'clock, with your night-cap in your pocket."

The latter precaution was not unnecessary, for the insatiable host (after the evening's entertainment was over and the guests gone home) would not consent to release his young *protégé* under at least half-a-dozen of Bach's fugues for a "good-night," or "*evening blessing*," as he was wont to call it.

Most valuable were the evenings spent in Van Swieten's house to Beethoven, for here he was first made fully acquainted with the majesty of Handel, "that unequalled master of all masters," in Beethoven's estimation, of whom he once said: "Go, and learn of him how to produce, with small means, such great effects!"

Another patron of the young musician, and one able to benefit him more substantially, was the Prince Karl Lichnowski, the accomplished pupil of Mozart, who, with his amiable wife Christiane, devoted every leisure hour to artistic pursuits. This couple, worthy in all respects of their exalted rank, at first attracted by the wonderful improvisation of Haydn's pupil, soon discovered, on a more intimate acquaintance, the true nobility of soul and dazzling genius which lay beneath the rough exterior.

They were childless; with the utmost delicacy it was proposed to Beethoven in 1794 that he should come to them; he accepted the offer in the spirit in which it was made, and for about ten years was an inmate of the Lichnowski Palace, treated with more than parental tenderness by the Prince and Princess. The latter took the place of Madame von Breuning, and Beethoven used afterwards to say laughingly, "They wanted to train me there with *grandmotherly* love; and the Princess Christiane would have liked to put a glass case over me, so that no evil might come nigh me."

Not that there was never any misunderstanding between Beethoven and his patron; on the contrary, the Princess had very often to mediate between them. How could it be otherwise? it was not easy for the powerful, impulsive mind of Beethoven, with his previous training, to accommodate itself to the smooth, etiquette-trammelled life of a palace. To abide by a settled routine was to him impossible; and after a few ineffectual struggles the attempt to make him do so was abandoned, and the artist left free to develop himself in his own way.

Wegeler relates that when he came to Vienna he found Beethoven installed in the Lichnowski Palace, but by no means so content with his position as one would imagine. Amongst other things he complained to him that the Prince's dinner-hour was fixed at four o'clock. "Now," said he, "I ought to be at home by half-past three to dress and trim my beard, &c. I could not stand that!" So some restaurant was more frequently honoured by his presence than the Lichnowski dinner-table.

It must not be thought that Beethoven forfeited any of his independence by thus becoming an inmate of the palace. On the contrary, he knew well, and the Prince did also, that the advantage was mutual. If he had a zealous and wealthy patron, the Prince had in return the benefit of the constant presence of the first pianist and improvisatore of the day at all his *Musikabende*, besides the *éclat* attached to the fact that so many of the composer's productions were first performed at his house. Not that either of them ever coolly balanced the one set of advantages over against the other. This was in point of fact the relation between them; in reality it was more like that of father and son.

The critical judgment of the Prince was highly esteemed by Beethoven, who often allowed himself to be persuaded by him into making alterations which no other influence had power to effect; and his proficiency as a pianoforte-player, which enabled him to master with comparative ease the difficulties in the new style inaugurated by his *protégé*, confirmed Beethoven in his own views, and gave him fresh strength to resist those who would have had him adopt a more simple manner of writing.

Beethoven's independence of thought and action was of vital importance in his development. "Help thyself!" was his motto. But we are sometimes inclined to smile at the lengths to which he carried his favourite doctrine. For instance, having overheard the prince (who had a peculiarly loud voice) direct his Jäger, that whenever Beethoven and he rang at the same time, the latter should be waited on first; he took care that very day to procure a servant for himself. Another time, when he had a great desire to learn riding, and the Prince's stud had been placed at his disposal, he would not accept the offer, but bought an animal for his own special use. Any one who has ever been so unlucky as to borrow a friend's favourite horse, will not find Beethoven's conduct in this instance so very peculiar.

We can now imagine our master settled for a time, in the possession of much that could make life enjoyable. His days were entirely at his own disposal, and generally occupied by study; his evenings were passed either in his patron's *salon*, at Van Swieten's, or at the house of some connoisseur. Wherever he went, he was welcomed, in spite of his unpolished manner and appearance.

We have seen how, rather than submit to the necessity of an elaborate toilette, he would content himself with the plainest fare; but there was that in Beethoven's *physique* which the utmost pains could never have smoothed down to the conventional standard. Rather short, with a figure more indicative of strength than elegance, hair that baffled Figaro's efforts to reduce it to order, and a broad face, whose one redeeming point was the lofty, expansive forehead—a true throne of genius—Beethoven presented a *tout-ensemble* which at once marked him out from all others, and was an index to the independent, original spirit within.

His demeanour was such as might be expected in one who had made his own life-path, and had constantly encountered hostility and misunderstanding; brusque, angular, and a little defiant; but—where he was sure of his ground—gentle and loveable as a woman, innocent and guileless as a child..

Beethoven had no time for the *petits-soins* of life, his thoughts were too deeply engrossed with higher matters, but that he was the bear so often represented, we emphatically deny. Such accusations were brought against him by those who were incapable of appreciating either him or his works, who would have had the great poet descend to the common level of everyday life, fritter away precious time and thought, and force his powerful mind to the punctilious observance of every little social etiquette.

One condition alone was necessary for Beethoven to come out in a favourable light in society, viz., *he must be understood.* Not flattered, not admired, not caressed,—simply understood in his true character as a poet, an artist, a revealer of beauty undreamt of by others. The following anecdote is an illustration of this :—

"When we were both still young (writes Herr von Griesinger, Ambassador from the Court of Saxony to Vienna), I only an *attaché*, and Beethoven only a celebrated pianoforte player, but as yet little known as a composer, we happened to be both together at the house of Prince Lobkowitz. A gentleman, who thought himself a great connoisseur, entered into a conversation with Beethoven upon a poet's life and inclinations. 'I wish,' said Beethoven, with his native candour, 'that I was relieved from all the bargain and sale of publication, and could meet with some one who could pay me a certain income for life, for which he should possess the right to publish exclusively all that I wrote; and I would not be idle in composition. I believe Goethe does this with Cotta, and, if I mistake not, Handel's London publisher held similar terms with him.'

"'My dear young man,' said this grave wiseacre, 'you must not complain, for you are neither a Goethe nor a Handel, and it is not to be expected that you ever will be, for such masters will not be born again.'"

"Beethoven bit his lips, gave a most contemptuous glance at the speaker, and said not another word to him. Afterwards, however, he expressed himself pretty warmly on the subject of this flippant individual.

"Prince Lobkowitz endeavoured to draw Beethoven into more temperate habits of thought, and said in a friendly manner, when the conversation once turned upon this person, 'My dear Beethoven, the gentleman did not intend to wound you; it is an established maxim, which most men adhere to, that the present generation cannot possibly produce such mighty spirits as the dead, who have already earned their fame.'

"'So much the worse, your Highness,' replied Beethoven; 'but with men who will not believe and trust in me because I am as yet unknown to universal fame, I cannot hold intercourse.'

"Many then shook their heads, and called the young composer arrogant and overbearing. Had these gentry been able to look into the future, they would have been a little ashamed of themselves."

With Beethoven's residence in the Lichnowski Palace, many characteristic anecdotes are connected, amongst others that already referred to of his reading the complicated Bach MS. *a prima vista.*

But one of the most important features of his life here was his connection with the Schuppanzigh Quartette, afterwards known as the Razoumowski, which, under his auspices, took so notable a place in musical annals. The players were all very young (Schuppanzigh, first violin, a boy of sixteen; Sina, second violin, still a very young man; Weiss, viola, fifteen; and Kraft, violoncello, only fourteen years of age), and this was probably a recommendation in the eyes of the Prince, who was passionately fond of the quartets of Haydn and Mozart, and doubtless found that he could more easily inoculate young and unformed minds with his peculiar views regarding the performance of them, than he could persuade more mature artists into adopting his views. Beethoven was his able coadjutor in this attempt, and the boy-quartet, directed by one not much older than themselves, did honour to the discernment of their patron. For many years they worked harmoniously together, meeting for practice every Friday morning, and probably no quartet-players, either before or since, enjoyed advantages so great. For them Beethoven composed his immortal productions, and his genius fired and animated theirs, so that one mind and one will alone seemed at work. The following note, preserved by Schindler, relative to the production of the difficult E. flat major Quartet in March, 1825, shows how his desire that his old companions should prove equal to their reputation continued unabated to the last :—

"My good Friends,—Herewith each will receive his part, and must with it promise allegiance, and pledge himself in all honour to do his very best to distinguish himself, and to vie with the others in zeal.

"Every one who wishes to take part in the affair must sign this paper."

(Here follow the four signatures.)

On one occasion a new pianoforte quartet by Forster, a well-known composer of the day, was in progress of rehearsal. The violoncellist was suddenly called out, when Beethoven, who was at the pianoforte, instantly began to sing the missing part in addition to going on with his own, which he read for the first time.

The Prince, astonished, asked him how he could sing music with which he was not acquainted. Beethoven smiled and replied, "The bass *must* have been so, otherwise the author could have known nothing whatever of composition." On the Prince remarking further, that Beethoven had taken the *Presto* so quickly that it was impossible for him to have seen the notes, he answered, "That is not at all necessary. A multitude of faults in the printing do not signify. If you only know the language, you don't see them or pay any heed to them."

To show the good understanding between Beethoven and the Princess Christiane, we give the following anecdote here, although it properly belongs to a later period.

One evening, Ries, while still Beethoven's pupil, in performing a sonata before a large company, played a wrong note, on which the master tapped him on the head with one finger by way of reminder. Beethoven next took his seat at the pianoforte, and the Princess (who always felt for the weak, and had observed that Ries was rather vexed by the occurrence) stationed herself behind the composer. Beethoven played the beginning of one of his own compositions rather carelessly, as he was often wont to do in commencing, when the Princess seized her opportunity, and giving him several well-directed blows, said : "When a pupil is punished with one finger for having failed in a single note, the master deserves to be punished with the whole hand for graver faults!" "Everybody began to laugh," adds Ries, "and Beethoven the first. He recommenced, and played admirably."

In the year 1793, the first of that unparalleled series of works which ended only in 1827 with Beethoven's death—the three Trios for pianoforte, violin, and Cello, Op. I.,—were publicly performed; that is to say, before a large and brilliant assembly in the Lichnowski Palace. The result was most gratifying, alike to the composer and to his friends—Beethoven was at once recognised as the successor of Mozart. One incident alone detracted from the happiness of the young author—Haydn, who was present, while warmly praising the two first trios, strongly recommended that the last, in C. minor, should not be published.

Beethoven's suspicion, already on the alert, was fairly roused by this apparently well-meaning advice. Why should that particular trio be kept back? He himself thought it the best and most original of the three, and as such it is now generally regarded.

It offered, however, such a contrast to his own simple style of trio-writing, that Haydn was, perhaps, honest in stating as his reason for advocating its non-publication that he did not believe the public would understand it. Beethoven, however, was strengthened by this occurrence in his conviction that Haydn "did not mean well by him;" and, though he deferred to the criticism at the time (probably more out of regard to Lichnowski's representations) a bitter feeling towards his former master rankled in his heart. This did not prevent his dedicating the three Pianoforte Sonatas, Op. II., to Haydn. The dedication, however, was a mere mark of appreciation, not of the man, but of his works, a compliment from one artist to the other—not a grateful recognition of the master by the pupil. In fact, when Haydn wished him to inscribe on the title-page, "Pupil of Haydn," he flatly refused, saying that he " had never learned anything from him!"

We have said that he deferred to Haydn's criticism, but he went beyond it. If the C. minor trio was not to be published, neither should the other two. So the unlucky works were thrust back into his portfolio, where they lay for two years, during which the irate composer paved the way for their proper reception by publishing an immense number of bagatelles, especially variations on different themes, which have no great value beyond that attached to them as studies in the development of Beethoven's genius.

Although evincing more ingenuity and variety than the themes treated by Mozart in the same way, they are often found unequal to the latter in clearness.* Beethoven seems to have had a lingering partiality for this style of writing. After having abandoned it, we find it adopted again in the Thirty-two Variations Sérieuses on an original theme, which were written after he had more than established his success in the Sonata form; and, so anxious was he to have them

* Marx, vol. i., p. 66.

well understood and rendered, that he made Ries, when studying them with him, repeat the last no fewer than seventeen times before he was satisfied with the effect; "though," adds Ries rather naïvely, "I thought I played it as well as Beethoven himself!"

The growth of the Thirty-three Variations, Op. 120, we must leave to Schindler to relate:—

"In the villa of Hetzendorf, Beethoven wrote the Thirty-three Variations on a Waltz by Diabelli, a work which delighted him uncommonly. At first there were only to be six or seven variations, for which modest number Diabelli had offered him eighty ducats (the price he received for almost each of his later Sonatas). But when he set to work, there sprang into life first ten, then twenty, then twenty-five—and still he could not stop. When Diabelli heard of the twenty-five variations, he was greatly concerned lest the work should be too large, but was at last obliged to accept for his eighty ducats, not *seven*, but *three and thirty variations*." The following story is a proof of the ease with which he invented variations. Being one evening in a box with a lady during a performance of "La Molinare," she lamented to him that she had once possessed a number of variations on the air "Nel cor non più mi sento," which she had lost. Next morning she received "Sei variazioni perdute per la—ritrovate per Luigi v. Beethoven."

The year 1795 brought with it two events; one the arrival of his brothers in Vienna: the other his first appearance in public as a virtuoso. Hitherto his performances had been confined to the Lichnowski

Palace, and other private houses, and public curiosity had long been whetted by the various rumours which flew about concerning him. At length it was to be gratified, on the occasion of the Annual Concert for the Widows and Orphans of Musicians. The direction of this was usually entrusted to Salieri, who held the *bâton* at the Italian Opera-house, and his programme for the year 1795 consisted of an operetta, composed by one of his pupils, and a Pianoforte Concerto in C. major by another, Herr Louis van Beethoven.

Wegeler relates that two days before the date fixed for the event the Concerto was not yet finished, and there did not seem much probability of its being ready in time, as Beethoven was suffering much from attacks of colic, to which he was often subject. Wegeler, from his medical knowledge, was able to render a little assistance, and so the work progressed, Beethoven writing as fast as he could, and handing over each sheet as it was finished to four copyists who were in attendance in the antechamber. Next day, at the rehearsal, the pianoforte was found to have been tuned half a tone lower than the other instruments; when Beethoven, to save time, played the whole Concerto through in the key of C. sharp!

Seyfried tells us that when Beethoven asked him to turn over the leaves of several of his concertos for him while playing in public, he found nothing but a sheet of paper with here and there a bar filled in, or a mass of notes unintelligible to any one but the composer. Jahn describes Mozart as doing the same, but what a difference is there between his concertos and—say, *the Emperor!*

The year 1797 was marked by a slight variation; Beethoven made a short journey to Berlin and Leipzig, the only occasion, with the exception of his visit to the Baths, on which he ever left Vienna or its neighbourhood. In both cities he met with a flattering reception. In Berlin he played his two sonatas for pianoforte and 'cello, Op. 5, before Frederick William II., who presented him with a snuff-box filled with Friedrichs-d'or; "not an ordinary snuff-box," as Beethoven was wont to remark with grim satisfaction, "but one similar to those given to ambassadors!"

Here, also, he unwittingly incurred the enmity of the pianist Himmel. The latter had begged Beethoven for an improvisation, with which request our musician complied, and then asked Himmel to favour him in return. Nothing loath, Himmel seated himself at the pianoforte and began a succession of smooth running passages and arpeggios, skilfully linked together. Beethoven listened for a while in silence, imagining this to be the prelude, but as it seemed to "go on for ever," he said with some impatience, "Pray do begin now!" Himmel, however had already exhausted his imagination and finished his (*quasi*) improvisation.

No better fate awaited others who opposed themselves to Beethoven as improvisatori, not excepting the celebrated pianists Woelfl and Steibelt. That the former could ever have been seriously regarded as the rival of Beethoven is scarcely credible to us. Such was the case, however, and as with Gluck and Picini in Paris, and Handel and Buononcini in London (connected with which Swift's well-known *jeu-d'esprit* will occur to every amateur), so it was with Beethoven and Woelfl in Vienna. Each had his allies, and party spirit ran so high that Beethoven, although devoid of any feeling of rivalry, accepted a challenge to improvise. The meeting took place at the villa of Baron von Wetzlar, Woelfl's patron; the pianofortes were placed side by side, and the two artists played and improvised by turns.

Inspired by the ardour of contest, each seemed to surpass himself; never had Woelfl's technical skill seemed greater; never had the wealth of Beethoven's ideas shone out more resplendently. Some of Woelfl's stoutest adherents contended that he had gained the day in a technical point of view, and this may, perhaps, have been the case, since his immense hand, which enabled him to grasp tenths with the same ease as octaves, undoubtedly gave him an advantage. His sonata, "Non plus ultra," gives us an idea of his execution.

Beethoven, on the other hand, never cared to make a display of mere dash and brilliancy; technicalities were always subordinated by him to idea and feeling.

The gift of improvisation must have been his to an extent unparalleled either before or since. His wealth of idea, certainty of form, and poetry of expression, combined to produce an effect very different from that achieved by ordinary extempore players, who in general, as we have seen in the case of Himmel, mistook the art of preluding for that of improvising. Only one conversant with that language of music to which Beethoven often alluded, could venture, without preparation, to speak to any purpose in it.

A circumstance that contributed to his success was his *power of abstraction*, which, in common with all deep thinkers, he possessed in a remarkable degree. With the first few bars of the given Thema, the scene before his eyes, the daylight, the bystanders, all vanished; and Beethoven was as fully immersed in the solitude of his own thoughts as though he had been suddenly transported to some desert island, with penguins and sea-gulls for listeners.

Ries gives a curious instance of this utter disregard of all outward things, in the story of the great master's commencing one day, while giving him a lesson, to play with the left hand the first fugue from Graun's "Tod Jesu." Gradually the right hand was added, and regardless of his awkward position, the fugue developed in all conceivable manners for the space of half an hour, when he suddenly awoke to discover that his pupil was still in his place before the pianoforte.

In 1798 a more formidable rival appeared at Vienna in the person of Steibelt. Having conceived a great idea of his own powers from the flattery of his Parisian admirers, Steibelt came to the capital sure of conquest, and did not even consider it necessary to visit the opponent so far beneath him. They met accidentally at the house of Count Fries, "where," says Ferdinand Ries, "Beethoven played for the first time his Trio in B. flat major for piano, clarionet, and 'cello, Op. 11, in which there is not much room for display.

"Steibelt heard it with a kind of condescension, payed Beethoven several compliments, and believed himself sure of victory. He played a quintet of his own composition, and then improvised and produced a great sensation by his free use of the shake, which was at that time something quite new.

"To ask Beethoven to play again was not to be thought of.

"Eight days after there was again a concert at Count Fries. Steibelt played another quintet with great success; he had besides, as might be easily perceived, *studied* a brilliant improvisation, and chosen for a subject the same theme on which the finale of Beethoven's trio was built. This disgusted the admirers of Beethoven, and displeased the latter also. It was his turn to seat himself at the pianoforte and to improvise. He placed himself at the instrument with his ordinary air—I might say, rather ill-humouredly, and as if pushed there. In passing he seized the violoncello part of Steibelt's quintet, placed it upside down on the desk (was this designedly?), and drummed out with one finger the theme of the first few bars.

"Then, impelled by his insulted and excited feelings, he improvised in such a manner that Steibelt quitted the room before Beethoven had ceased. He would never meet him again, and, when invited anywhere, always stipulated that Beethoven should not be present."

But enough of such anecdotes! Triumphs which would have been glory to others were nothing to him. Let us pass on and see the master in the great struggle which prefaced the real commencement of life's work, and was continued without intermission until the victory was won.

CHAPTER VI.

CONFLICT.

Deafness and its Consequences—His Brothers' Influence—Letters to Wegeler—"Mount of Olives"—Beethoven's Will—Beethoven as an Instructor—a Conductor—Sinfonia Eroica—"Leonora" ("Fidelio")—"Adelaïde."

SUFFERING and genius! apparently so far apart, in reality so near!
The bitter cry of Milton,—

"Dark, dark, dark, amidst the blaze of noon!"

has gone up from many a thousand hearts to the eternal throne; but who may presume to fathom the dispensations of a mysterious providence? or to question that wisdom which gives to every earthborn soul the necessary discipline for immortality? Let us rather wonder and adore, and—

"Know how sublime a thing it is
To suffer and *be strong.*"

We left our young musician in the full flush of success, in apparently vigorous health, caressed and flattered by princes, without a rival as a virtuoso, and fast leaving all competitors behind him as a composer, when suddenly a cloud appears, the brightness is overcast, and darkness comes on apace. *Beethoven became deaf.*

For three years he had had premonitory fears, which were too sadly realized in the year 1800.

The loss of hearing is deprivation enough in ordinary cases; but to a young man of excitable artist temperament, and a musician! it seemed for a while worse than the loss of life itself. Our Beethoven writes thus to Wegeler:—

"If I had not read somewhere that man must not of his own free will depart this life, I should long ere this have been no more, and that through my own act."

From this despair he was mercifully rescued. The strong, secret voice within, impelling Beethoven onwards and upwards to that aim which he "felt, but could not describe," spoke now in more stirring accents and with more thrilling emphasis amid the profound silence and desolation of his nature.

He "was not disobedient" to the heavenly call; the triumph of mind was achieved; and from the dark prison-house the noblest strains the world has ever heard escaped to wake responsive echoes in the hearts of all who have felt and suffered.

But this victory was not gained without leaving behind it evident tokens of the struggle; distrust, suspicion, irritability, those constant attendants on deafness, haunted Beethoven day and night, poisoning his happiness, and casting their shadow over his childlike, benevolent disposition. Stephan Breuning writes thus of the alteration in his friend in a letter dated the 13th of November, 1806 :—"You cannot realize the indescribable impression made upon Beethoven by the loss of his hearing. Imagine, with his excitable temperament, the feeling of unhappiness, added to reserve, distrust of his best friends, and indecision in many things. In general, intercourse with him is a positive exertion, in which it is impossible to feel entirely at one's ease ; the occasions on which his old true nature shows itself are few indeed."

Schindler, also his friend and biographer, describes him as being "like a child, devoid of all experience, suddenly cast upon this earth from some ideal world ; like a ball, tossed from one hand to another ; consequently, at the mercy of other people. And," he adds, "*so Beethoven remained throughout his whole life.*"

These evils were increased by the presence of his brothers, Carl and Johann (the "evil principles" of his life, as Schindler calls them), who now began to exercise an almost unlimited influence over him. These men seem to have been totally incapable of appreciating the true character or work of Ludwig ; they only saw that he was making money rapidly (and, as they thought, easily), and determined to take advantage of it. To this end they resolved to obtain entire possession of him, and began by endeavouring to alienate as far as possible Beethoven's friends, misrepresenting to him all that occurred, and fanning every little spark of anger into a flame.

Their efforts partially succeeded; our unhappy composer, absorbed in his own creations, overwhelmed by his misfortune, and intensely irritable, was but too ready to believe all the world in league against him, and would have shut the door against his best friends. Prince Lichnowski alone had still some weight with him, and when once persuaded that he had acted unjustly, nothing could exceed Beethoven's contrition and desire to make amends to those he had wounded.

But he would never lay any blame upon his brothers, and even when their duplicity and falseness had been clearly pointed out to him, he would still continue to defend them strenuously, refusing to look upon their conduct in any but the most favourable light, and adding, "After all, they are my brothers."

It may easily be believed how, with dispositions such as those of Carl and Johann, this mistaken lenity and brotherly feeling confirmed them in their course. It was they who generally made all arrangements with the music publishers, and through their instrumentality many minor pieces were given to the world which the composer had produced in Bonn, and kept back from publication as unworthy of his name.

Such a consideration, however, had no weight with the two; money they wanted, and were resolved to get at all hazards. Once only did Beethoven come into collision with them regarding this, when he discovered that Carl had, without his knowledge, sold a copyright which had been promised to another person.

Carl held a situation in the National Bank of Austria, and Johann had been established by Beethoven as an apothecary. In a very short time, however, the latter became so wealthy (how?) as to be able to exchange the pestle and mortar for the state of a country gentleman. Of this he was so immoderately proud, that one New Year's day he sent in to his brother a card, on which was written,—

"Johann van Beethoven, Land Proprietor."

The composer, who was at table when it was brought to him, laughed heartily, and writing on the other side,—

"Ludwig van Beethoven, Brain Proprietor,"

sent it back to him.

The following letters to Wegeler display, more fully than we can describe, Beethoven's condition during the first few years of his calamity :—

"*Vienna, 29th June,* 1800.

"MY DEAR GOOD WEGELER,—How much I thank you for your remembrance of me! I have deserved it, and sought to deserve it, so little ; and yet you are so good, and will not allow yourself to be discouraged even by my unpardonable neglect—you are always the same true, good, worthy friend. That

I could ever forget you or yours, who were once so dear and precious to me, do not believe; there are moments in which I long for you, and wish that it were in my power to spend some time with you. My fatherland, the lovely spot in which I first saw the light, is as distinct and beautiful before my eyes now as when I first left you. In short, I shall consider it one of the happiest events of my life when I am able to see you, and to greet our Father Rhine again. When this will be I cannot positively say. So much I will tell you—you shall not see me again until I have become really great—not as an artist only, but a better and more perfect man: and if the prosperity of my country be once more re-established, my art shall be devoted solely to the relief of the poor. Oh blissful moment! how happy do I consider myself in being able to procure thee—to create thee!

"You want to know something about my position? Well, after all it is not so bad. Lichnowski is still, and always has been, my warmest friend, however incredible it may appear to you. (Of course there were little misunderstandings between us; but did they not serve rather to cement our friendship?) Since last year he has settled on me a pension of six hundred guldens, which I am to draw until I find an appointment suited to me. I make a great deal by my compositions; indeed, I may say that there are more demands upon me than I can execute. For every one of my works I have at least six or seven publishers, and could have more if I wished. They do not drive bargains with me now: I demand, and they pay. You see this is a very good thing. If, for instance, I see a friend in difficulty, and am not in funds to help him immediately, I have only to sit down and write, and in a short time he is relieved. I am also more economical than I used to be. If I remain here permanently, I shall certainly contrive to reserve one day in every year for a grand concert, of which I have already given several. That malicious demon, bad health, has cast a stumblingblock in my path—for the last three years my hearing has gradually become weaker. The original cause of this defect is the state of my digestive organs, which, as you know, was formerly bad enough, but has now become much worse, for I have been constantly troubled with diarrhœa, which has induced extreme weakness. Frank tried to restore the tone to my constitution by strengthening medicines, and to my hearing by oil of almonds, but *prosit!* with no good effect; my hearing grew worse, and my digestion remained in the same state. This lasted till the autumn of last year, and I was often in despair. Then one medical *asinus* recommended cold bathing for my complaint; another, a little more sensible, the ordinary tepid Danube bath. This worked wonders; my digestion became better, but my deafness continued as bad as ever, or grew worse. Last winter I was truly miserable, suffering so dreadfully from colic that I fell completely back again into my former state, in which I continued till about four weeks ago, when I went to consult Vering;* partly

* Surgeon-in-Chief to the army.

because I think my complaint requires surgical treatment, and partly also because I have always had confidence in him. He succeeded in almost entirely arresting the violent diarrhœa. He ordered me the tepid Danube bath, into which I pour every time a phial of some strengthening mixture; but he gave me no medicine at all, except four days ago some digestive pills and a lotion for the ears. I must say I find myself much stronger and better for this treatment, but the buzzing and ringing in my ears continues day and night.

"I may say that I pass my life wretchedly; for nearly two years I have avoided all society, because I cannot possibly say to people, '*I am deaf!*' If I were in any other profession it would not so much signify, but for a musician it is a really frightful condition. Besides, what would my enemies say to it? —and they are not few!

"To give you an idea of this extraordinary deafness, I must tell you that in the theatre I am obliged to lean forward quite close to the orchestra in order to understand the actors. The high tones of the instruments and voices I do not hear if I am a little way off. In conversation it is surprising that there are some people who do not observe it—they attribute it to the absent fits which I often have. Many a time I can with difficulty distinguish the tones, but not the words, of any person who speaks in a low voice; and yet, directly any one begins to shout, it is unendurable to me. What is to be the result of all this, the good God alone knows. Vering says that my condition will certainly improve, though I may not be perfectly restored. I have often already—cursed my existence. Plutarch has led me to resignation. I am resolved, if possible, to defy my fate, although there should be moments in my life when I shall be the most unhappy of all God's creatures.

"I beg of you not to mention my state to any one, not even to Lorchen ;* I only confide it as a secret to you. I should like much if you would correspond some day with Vering about it. Should my affliction continue, I shall come next spring to you. You shall hire a house for me in some lovely spot in the country, and there I shall become a peasant for six months. Perhaps that might bring about a change. Resignation! what a miserable refuge! and yet the only one left to me!

"You must forgive me for adding the burden of these friendly cares to your troubles, already gloomy enough. Steffen Breuning† is now here, and we are almost every day together; it does me so much good to call up the old feelings. He has become really a capital fellow, who knows something, and has his heart pretty much in the right place, like us all.

"I have very pleasant rooms now close to the Ramparts,‡ which is doubly advantageous for my health. I think I shall be able to manage so that Breuning may come to me.

* Eleanore von Breuning.   † Stephan von Breuning.
‡ Probably in the house of Baron Pasqualati.

"Your Antiochus* you shall have, together with plenty of music from me,—that is, if you do not fear its costing you too much. Honestly, your love of art rejoices me greatly. Only let me know how to set about it, and I shall send you all my works, which now amount to a pretty number, and are daily added to.

"Instead of the portrait of my grandfather (which I beg you to send me as soon as possible with the mail), I send you that of his grandson, your ever loving and affectionate Beethoven. It has been brought out here by Artaria, who, as well as other publishers, has often begged me for it. I shall write next to Stoffeln†, and read him a lecture about his peevish temper. I shall sound our old friendship well in his ears, and get him to promise sacredly not to annoy you again in your present sad position.

"Never have I forgotten one of you, my dear, good friends, although I may not have written often to you; but writing, as you know, was never my *forte;* even my best friends have not heard from me for years. I live only in my music; and, no sooner is one thing completed, than another is begun. In fact, as at present, I am often engaged on three or four compositions at one time.

"Write me now frequently; I shall make a point of finding time to write you occasionally. Give my kind regards to all, especially to the good Frau Hofräthin‡, and tell her that even now I sometimes have a 'raptus.'

* A painting by Füger, Director of the Vienna Academy.
† Christoph Breuning. ‡ Madame von Breuning.

"With regard to K——, I am not at all surprised at the change. Fortune rolls on like a ball; and naturally, therefore, does not always stop at what is noblest and best. One word for Ries,* to whom remember me cordially. With regard to his son,† I shall write you more particularly, but I believe that Paris offers a better field for his exertions than Vienna, which is so overstocked that even people of the greatest merit find it a hard matter to maintain themselves. By autumn or winter I shall see what I can do for him, for then everybody will have returned to town.

"Farewell, my good, faithful Wegeler. Rest assured of the love and friendship of your
"BEETHOVEN."

Vienna, November 16th, 1801.

"MY DEAR WEGELER,—For this fresh proof of your solicitude about me, I must thank you the more, that I deserve it so little. You want to know how I am progressing, and what remedies I use; however unwilling I am in general to refer to this subject, I do so with the least reluctance to you.

"For several months past, Vering has ordered me to apply blisters constantly to both arms, made of a certain kind of bark, which you doubtless know. This is a most disagreeable remedy, inasmuch as

---
* Franz Ries, the violinist.
† Ferdinand, afterwards Beethoven's pupil.

(without taking the pain into consideration) I am deprived of the free use of my arms for a few days, until the blisters have drawn sufficiently. It is true, and I cannot deny it, that the buzzing and ringing are somewhat less than formerly, especially in the left ear, that in which my malady first commenced —but my hearing is certainly not a whit better, I dare not say positively that it has not rather grown worse.

"My digestion is better, especially after using the tepid baths, when I feel tolerably well for eight or ten days. Tonics I very seldom take, but follow your advice now with regard to the herb-plasters. Plunge baths Vering will not hear of. On the whole, I am not at all pleased with him; he has far too little solicitude or indulgence for a malady such as mine; if I did not go to him, and this I cannot do without great difficulty, I should never see him. What do you think of Schmidt?* I am unwilling to make a change, but it seems to me that Vering is too much of a practitioner to gain fresh ideas by reading. With regard to this, Schmidt appears a very different sort of man, and might also, perhaps, not be quite so negligent of my case.

"I hear wonders of galvanism—what say you to it? A medical man told me that he had known a deaf and dumb child whose hearing was fully restored by it (in Berlin), and also a man who, after

---

* Professor of Medicine at the Académie Joséphine, and author of several works.

having been deaf for seven years, recovered his hearing. They tell me that your friend Schmidt is making experiments on the subject.

"I lead a somewhat more agreeable life now that I mingle more with other people. You can hardly realize what a miserable, desolate life mine has been for the last two years. Like a ghost did my deafness haunt me everywhere, till I fled society, and must have appeared a misanthrope—yet this is so little my character.

"This change has been brought about by a lovely and fascinating girl,* who loves me, and whom I love. After the lapse of two years I have again enjoyed some blissful moments, and now for the first time I feel that marriage can bestow happiness; but, alas! she is not in the same rank of life as myself; and at present, certainly I could not marry: I must first bestir myself actively. Were it not for my deafness, I would long ago have travelled half round the world, and I must do it yet. For me there is no greater pleasure than to follow and promote my art. Do not believe that I could be happy with you. What would there be, indeed, to make me happier? Even your solicitude would pain me; every moment I should read sympathy on your faces, and should find myself only the more wretched.

"Those lovely scenes of my Fatherland, what part had I in them? Nothing but the hope of a better future, which would have been mine, were it not for

---

* Undoubtedly the Countess Julia Guicciardi.

this affliction! Oh! once free from this, I would span the world! My youth, I feel it, is only beginning; have I not always been a sickly creature? For some time past my bodily strength has been increasing more than ever, and my mental power as well. Every day I approach nearer the goal which I feel, but cannot describe. Only in this can your Beethoven live. No rest for me! I know of none other than Sleep, and sorry enough I am to be obliged to give up more time to it than formerly. Let me be only half delivered from this malady, and then—a more perfect, mature man—I shall come to you, and renew the old feelings of friendship.

"You shall see me as happy as I am destined to be here below,—not unhappy. No, that I could not bear. I will grasp Fate by the throat, it shall not utterly crush me. Oh! it is so glorious to live one's life a thousand times! For a quiet life, I feel it, I am no longer made.

"Pray do write me as soon as possible. Persuade Steffen to decide upon seeking an appointment somewhere from the Teutonic Order.* His position here is too fatiguing for his health, and besides, he leads such an isolated life, that I do not see how he is ever to get on. You know how things are here. I will not positively say that society would lessen his de-

---

* The Breuning family had long been in possession of one of the most honourable posts in the Teutonic Order, four members had successively filled the office of Chancellor, and Stephan himself was afterwards appointed to the government of Mergentheim. He was generally esteemed, and died a short time after Beethoven.

pression, but we cannot persuade him to join in it at all. A short time ago I had some music in my house, but our friend Steffen stayed away. Advise him to be more calm and composed. I have already tried all my powers on him,—without this he can never be either happy or in good health. Tell me in your next letter if there is any objection to my sending you my music, even though there should be a quantity of it. What you don't require, you can sell, and thus get back what you paid for carriage,—and my portrait into the bargain.

"Say all that is kind and obliging to Lorchen, as well as to her mamma and Christoph. Have you still a little love for me? Be convinced of the love as well as of the friendship of

"Your
BEETHOVEN."

The year 1800 found Beethoven already busy with his "Mount of Olives," which, however, was not produced till 1803. This, the master's first and last attempt at oratorio writing, "is a striking instance of the insufficiency of even the highest powers to accomplish that to which the special call has not been given. It was impossible for Beethoven to feel himself so inspired by his task as the composer of a time when the mind of the people was almost exclusively occupied by religious convictions; the man of the revolutionary period could not see or think out a Christ like that of Bach and Handel before him. Even the pure spring, out of which we Protestants of the eighteenth and nineteenth centuries draw our ideas of Christ—the Bible—flowed not for him; his Christ must first be poetically made for him. And how? The poet had no other aim but that of making verses for a composer; the latter no other motive than the ordinary creative impulse prompting him to try his powers in a different and important sphere. The result on both sides could not, therefore, be other than *Phrases*, although the better of the two proceeded from the composer, and that composer was Beethoven. To conceal or palliate this would be derogatory to the reverence which we all owe to Beethoven,—he stands too high to be in need of extenuation."

So far Marx; but in addition to the miserable libretto (which imparted unreality, artificiality, to the whole work, and especially gave to the part of the Saviour a theatrical air which Beethoven afterwards deplored) many peculiarities of the oratorio—with all deference to the able critic just quoted—may be traced to the period in which it was composed. The very choice of subject reveals the convulsion that was taking place in Beethoven's *volcanic* nature. It is a question whether Beethoven would ever have asserted his sovereignty in this branch of composition; it may be, as Marx hints, that the peculiar tone of thought and feeling necessary to the successful treatment of sacred subjects was wanting in him; but there can be no doubt that had the master's attention been devoted to the subject in happier days, when his tempest-tossed nature had attained to some degree of peace and serenity, the result would have been very different. Let him who would see Beethoven as a *devotional* writer, turn to his Gellert songs, which breathe the very depths of true religious feeling.

The greater part of the oratorio, and also of "Fidelio," was composed at Hetzendorf, a pretty little village near the imperial summer palace of Schönbrunn. Here Beethoven passed several summers in the greatest retirement—wandering all day long, from early dawn to nightfall, amid the leafy glades of the park. His favourite seat was between two immense boughs of an old oak, which branched out from the parent stem about two feet from the ground. This memorable tree, endeared to Beethoven as the birthplace of many a thought, was afterwards visited by him, in Schindler's company, in 1823.

In 1802 a gleam of hope dawned upon the sufferer; his deafness was for a time cured by the skilful treatment of Dr. Schmidt (to whom, out of gratitude, he dedicated his Septet arranged as a Trio), by whose advice he went for the summer to the village of Heiligenstadt, in the hope that the calm, sweet influence of nature, to which he was at all times most sensitive, might act beneficially upon his troubled mind.

This spot—this *consecrated town*—must always be an object of veneration to those who cherish the name of Beethoven, for here it was that he wrote his remarkable will, or promemoria, a document which excites our warmest sympathy, revealing, as it does, the depths of that great heart.

"To my Brothers, Carl and —— Beethoven.*—O ye who consider or represent me as unfriendly, morose, and misanthropical, how unjust are you to me! you know not the secret cause of what appears thus to you.

"My heart and mind have been from childhood given up to the tender feeling of benevolence, and I have ever been disposed to accomplish something great. But only consider that for six years I have been afflicted by a wretched calamity, which was aggravated by unskilful physicians—deceived from year to year by the hope of amendment—now forced, at length, to the contemplation of a *lingering disease* (the cure of which will, perhaps, last for years, if indeed it be not an impossibility).

"Born with a passionate, lively temperament, keenly susceptible to the pleasures of society, I was obliged at an early age to isolate myself, and to pass my life in loneliness.

"When I at times endeavoured to surmount all this, oh, how rudely was I thrust back again by the experience—the doubly painful experience—of my defective hearing! and yet it was impossible for me to say to people, Speak louder, shout; for I am deaf! Alas! how could I proclaim the weakness of a sense which ought to have been with me in a higher degree

---

* The omission of the name of Johann may be accounted for in two ways, viz., either Beethoven himself left it out purposely, through irritation at his conduct; or it was withheld by those who first published the document, out of respect to Johann's feelings, he being still alive.

than with others—a sense which I once possessed in the greatest perfection—and to an extent which few of my profession enjoy, or ever have enjoyed! Oh, this I cannot do! Forgive me, therefore, when you see me turn away where I would gladly mingle with you. My misfortune is doubly painful to me, inasmuch as it causes me to be misunderstood. For me there can be no relaxation in human society, no refined conversations, no mutual outpourings of thought. Like an exile must I live. Whenever I come near strangers, I am seized with a feverish anxiety from my dread of being exposed to the risk of betraying my condition.

"Thus it has been with me during these last six months which I have spent in the country. The orders of my sensible physician, to spare my hearing as much as possible, were quite in accordance with my present disposition; although often, overcome by my longing for society, I have been tempted into it. But what humiliation, when any one by my side heard from afar a flute, and I heard *nothing*, or when any one heard *the shepherd singing*, and I again heard *nothiug*!

"Such occurrences brought me nigh to despair; but little was wanting, and I should myself have put an end to my existence. *Art*—art alone—held me back! Ah! it seemed impossible for me to quit the world before I had done all that I felt myself destined to accomplish. And so I prolonged this miserable life; a life so truly wretched that a sudden change is sufficient to throw me from the happiest condition into the

"*Patience!* it would seem that I must now choose her for my guide! I have done so. I trust that my resolve to persevere will remain firm, until it shall please the inexorable Fates to cut the thread of life. Perhaps I may get better; perhaps not. I am prepared. Compelled to be a philosopher in my twenty-eighth year!* This is not easy—for the artist harder than for any one else. O God! Thou lookest down upon my heart, Thou seest that love to man and beneficent feelings have their abode in it!

"O ye who may one day read this, reflect that you did me injustice, and let the unhappy be consoled by finding one like himself, who, in defiance of all natural obstacles, has done all that lay in his power to be received into the ranks of worthy artists and men.

"My brothers, Carl and ———, as soon as I am dead, if Professor Schmidt be still alive, beg him in my name to describe my disease, and then add these pages to the history of my malady, that at least, so far as possible, the world may be reconciled to me after my death.

"I also hereby declare you both heirs of my little fortune (if so it may be called). Divide it honestly, bear with and help one another. What you did against me I have, as you know, long since forgiven. I thank you in particular, brother Carl, for the attachment which you have shown me of late. My wish is,

---

* Beethoven was at the time in his thirty-second year; but he never knew precisely his age.

that your life may be happier, and more free from care, than mine has been. Recommend *Virtue* to your children ; it is she alone, and not money, that can confer happiness. I speak from experience ; for it was Virtue who raised me when in distress. I have to thank her, in addition to my art, that I did not put an end to my life through suicide. Farewell, and love one another! I thank all my friends, especially Prince Lichnowski and Professor Schmidt. I should like the instruments of Prince L. to be preserved by one of you ; but let no dispute arise between you on this account. As soon as you perceive that it will be more to your advantage, you have only to sell them. How shall I rejoice, if even in the grave I can serve you!

"Thus has it happened :—with joy I hasten to meet Death. Should he come before I have had opportunity to develop all my artistic powers, he will have come too soon, notwithstanding my hard fate, and I shall wish that he had tarried a little longer ; but even then I shall be content, for he will set me free from a state of endless suffering. Come when thou wilt—I go courageously to meet thee!

"Farewell, and do not quite forget me even in death. I have deserved this of you, since in my life I often thought of you, and wished to make you happy.

"So be it!

"LUDWIG VAN BEETHOVEN.

"*Heiligenstadt, 6th October,* 1802."

"*Heiligenstadt, 10th October, 1802.*

"Thus I bid farewell to thee, mournfully enough. Even the dearest hope that I brought hither with me, the hope of being to a certain degree restored, has utterly forsaken me. As the leaves of autumn fall and wither, so has my hope faded. Almost as I came do I depart; even the lofty courage which inspired me during the lovely days of summer has vanished. Oh, Providence! vouchsafe to me one more day of pure happiness! The responsive echo of pure joy has been so long a stranger to my heart. When, when, O God! shall I again feel it in the temple of nature and man? Never? Ah! that would be too hard!"

(On the outside.)
"For my brothers Carl and ——, to be read and fulfilled after my death."

Several writers have maintained that the consequences of Beethoven's deafness are plainly discernible in his compositions; that he lost all idea of harmonic relations, that his later works are mere incongruous, erratic fancies, devoid of form and melody, and, in short, compared to his former productions, what the second part of "Faust" is to the first.

Happily, such ideas—promulgated by theorists of the old school like Fétis, and dilettanti of the Mozart-Italian school like Oulibicheff—have now exploded, and the service rendered to Art by Beethoven's latest works—especially his pianoforte sonatas—is fully recognised. It is these which have brought the pianoforte to its present eminence as the most intellectual and ideal of all instruments, and which, by their depth of thought and loftiness of aim, have raised an insuperable barrier between the dilettante who trifles with music for amusement, and the artist who devotes his life to its cultivation as a God-appointed means of developing the divine in man.

At the same time we come upon passages here and there which Beethoven would, perhaps, have written otherwise, had his ear, as well as his mind, been sensitive to their effect.

It is not posterity that has been the loser by Beethoven's deafness; we, at least, ought to appreciate the "precious jewel" which his adversity carried within it, and has handed down to us. His contemporaries, however, had cause to lament, for in a few years it put a stop to all improvising and playing in public. We read, indeed, of a plan for an artistic tour with his pupil Ries, when the latter was to make all arrangements for concert-giving, and to play the pianoforte Concertos and other works, while Beethoven conducted and improvised—but the project never came to maturity. It was, in fact, impossible. Beethoven entirely lost the sensitiveness of touch which had once distinguished his playing from that of all contemporaries; and, in his efforts to extract some nourishment for his hungering ear, used to hammer the pianoforte so unmercifully as generally to break several strings. Nor could it be obviated by a special instrument constructed for himself, nor by a sound-conductor invented for him by the ingenious Graff.

A curious feature of his deafness was the gradual manner in which the auricular nerve decayed; he first lost the power of catching the higher notes of singers or instruments, as we have seen, while deep, low sounds were long audible to him; this may account for the prevalence of those deep-lying tones in almost all his later works, especially the Second Mass and the Ninth Symphony.

As a natural consequence of his affliction, he soon became unable to conduct his own orchestral works. This, however, was no great loss, for he had never possessed either the self-possession or the experience necessary to wield the *bâton* satisfactorily. Knowing thoroughly as he did what every instrument had to say, he listened excitedly for each in detail—without calmly attending to the effect of the whole; at each *crescendo* he would rise as if about to fly, gesticulating so rapidly and energetically that the members of the orchestra (who had enough to do to follow such new and peculiar music) were often more bewildered than guided by his directions. At the same time be it distinctly understood that, however low the performance might fall beneath his "ideal," however vexatious the mistakes of individual performers might be, he never lost his temper, or acted in the manner related by Ries in his Notices, of which the following is a specimen :—

"Beethoven was present at the first performance of his Fantasia for pianoforte, orchestra, and chorus.

The clarinettist, in a passage where the beautiful subject of the finale has already entered, made by mistake a repetition of eight bars. As very few instruments are heard at this point, the error in the execution was torturing to the ear. Beethoven rose furiously, turned round, and insulted the musicians in the grossest manner, and so loudly that it was heard by the whole audience. Then, resuming his seat, he exclaimed, "From the beginning!" The movement was recommenced, and this time all went well, and the success was brilliant. But when the concert was over, the artists recollected only too well the honourable titles by which Beethoven had publicly addressed them; and, as if the matter had but that moment occurred, became excessively angry, and vowed never to play again when Beethoven was in the orchestra, &c., &c."

That the clarinettist did make a mistake is true, but that Beethoven behaved in the outrageous way described was most positively denied by all who were present on the occasion, including the conductor, Franz Clement. Where Ries got the story from is difficult to imagine, since he was himself in St. Petersburg at the time. On the contrary, the members of the orchestra were all on excellent terms with Beethoven, who prized their approval far more than that of the general public; and was wont, when particularly pleased with a performance, to turn round, his face beaming with delight, and exclaim, "Bravi, tutti!" But woe betide those who dared to question the effect of the new and somewhat startling combinations which he introduced! Ries found this out to his cost. At the unexpected entrance of the horn in the Allegro of the Eroica, he—as usual, beside his master in the orchestra—exclaimed, "How abominably wrong!" for which outburst he was nearly rewarded by a box on the ear.

Pianoforte playing, improvisation, and orchestral conducting were given up one after the other—not suddenly, for Beethoven was resolved to defy his fate as long as possible,—but henceforth it is with Beethoven the composer alone that we have to do.

The autumn of 1802 saw him so far restored as to be able to commence his great work on Napoleon, which, however, on account of many interruptions, was not finished until the year 1804.

In 1802 he writes thus to his publisher, Hofmeister, who had requested him to compose a sonata of a revolutionary tendency :—"Are you riding to the devil in a body, gentlemen, that you propose to me to write *such a sonata?* At the time of the revolutionary fever it might have done, but now, when everything is once more in the beaten track, when Bonaparte has signed the Concordat with the Pope—now such a sonata! If it had been a *missa pro Sancta Maria a tre voci*, or a *Vesper*, I would immediately have taken pen in hand and written in ponderous notes a *Credo in unum*,—but, good heavens! such a sonata in these fresh, dawning Christian times! Ho! ho! I'll have nothing to do with it!" and yet at this very time he must have been busy with a work destined to the honour of the great Disturber of the Peace of Europe.

The idea for this emanated originally from General Bernadotte, the French Ambassador at Vienna—a great admirer of the composer,—and was in reality warmly entered into by Beethoven, who, with his red-hot Republicanism and love for Plato, was an enthusiastic supporter of the First Consul, and imagined nothing less than that it was Napoleon's intention to remodel France according to the Platonic method, and inaugurate a golden age of universal happiness. With the news of the empire came the destruction of this elysian prospect,—Beethoven in a fury tore to pieces the title-page of his symphony on which was written simply,—

"BONAPARTE.
"LUIGI V. BEETHOVEN;"

and stamping it under foot, showered a volley of imprecations on the head of the tyrant who had played so false a game.

No persuasion could induce him at first to publish the work, but after the lapse of some years this masterpiece of ideal writing was given to the world under the title of " Sinfonia Eroica per festegiare il sovvenire d'un grand' uomo." Great man as Napoleon had been in Beethoven's estimation, he never could think of him otherwise than with detestation, till the sudden collapse of the Napoleonic idea in 1815, and the death of its promoter in 1821, changed his wrath into a kind of grim commiseration, which he showed by remarking that he had "seventeen years before composed the music suited to this catastrophe!" meaning the Funeral March in the Eroica.

This, the first great manifesto of the Sovereign of the World of Sound, was a wonderful advance on the first two symphonies, produced somewhere about the years 1800—1802. In these he took up the art where Haydn and Mozart had left it; but, "though he could dally and tarry awhile with them, he would not remain with them;" his greater earnestness impelled him on to realms unknown to them, to conquest compared with which theirs faded into comparative insignificance.

In 1805 Ferdinand Ries left Vienna, after having enjoyed Beethoven's instruction for five years. He was, in fact, the only one whom Beethoven recognised as his pupil (with the exception of the Archduke Rudolph), and to him he entrusted the playing of his concertos, &c., for the first time, when no longer able to do so himself. The impressions which Ries has left in his Notices, of Beethoven as an instructor, are like his other statements, somewhat contradictory. In one place he declares that during the lessons the master was engaged in composition or some similar work at one end of the room, while he was playing at the other, and that he seldom sat down by him for half an hour at a time. Again, he says that Beethoven took extraordinary pains with him—sometimes extending the lesson over two hours, and making him repeat ten times—nay, oftener —any passage with which he was not quite satisfied. Probably the truth lies between these two extremes. Beethoven, who had no settled order in his life, could not be expected to be systematic in tuition; hence the impression of desultoriness left upon the mind of the pupil. A characteristic anecdote of this period is worth quoting.

"Beethoven," says Ries, "had given me the manuscript of his third concerto, that I might appear in public with it for the first time as his pupil; Beethoven conducted and turned over the pages for me. I had begged him to compose a cadenza for me, but he directed me to write one myself. He was satisfied with my composition, and altered little; but one brilliant and very difficult passage, which seemed to him too hazardous, I was to change. The easier one did not please me, and I could not make up my mind to play it in public. The critical moment arrived—Beethoven had seated himself quietly—but when I boldly attacked the difficult cadence, he gave his chair a violent push. The cadenza, however, succeeded, and Beethoven was so delighted that he exclaimed, 'Bravo!' which electrified the audience."

In 1805 Beethoven produced his solitary opera, "Leonora" (afterwards known as "Fidelio"), amid a series of annoyances and vexations such as probably no operatic writer, either before or since, has ever had to contend against. What between troubles arising out of the libretto, the overture, the singers, the critics, and the theatrical cabals, our poor Beethoven was well-nigh driven distracted.

The story on which the opera is founded (originally taken from the French, and so well known as to require no repetition here) is almost too slight for dramatic purposes, inasmuch as there is but one really powerful situation—that of the grave scene—in the entire piece, and the whole interest, therefore, is concentrated on the one figure, Leonora. What Beethoven has made out of these slender materials; how he has depicted, in all its intensity and tenderness, that love which he was doomed never to experience, needs no description from us.

What was Beethoven's object in choosing this theme for his labours? Was it a foreshadowing of bliss that might be his? or was it the delineation of a character which, in its earnestness and purity, should be the reverse of that "Don Juan" of Mozart, of which he once said, "The divine art ought never to be lowered to the folly of such a scandalous subject"?

The little byplay and domestic "asides" cost our soaring Beethoven infinitely more trouble than the most impassioned scenas, and he was obliged to write the little air of Marcelline, "O, wär' ich schon mit Dir vereint," no less than thrice before he could attain the requisite lightness.

The composition of the four "Leonora" overtures is without a parallel in musical annals. When Beethoven had finished No. 1, in C major, he consented to its being first tried over by a small orchestra at Prince Lichnowski's, in the presence of a select number of critics and connoisseurs, by whom it was condemned as being light and almost flimsy in structure, and as affording no clue to the contents of the opera. It was therefore withdrawn, and not published till after the composer's death.

But may not the light-heartedness which distinguishes this overture have been intentional on the part of Beethoven? may he not have wished to represent his heroine before the shadow of grief had fallen upon her, in the enjoyment of the highest wedded bliss?

Marx takes this view of "Leonora" No. 1, adducing in support of it the following extract from one of the manuscript books in which Beethoven was accustomed to hold intercourse with his friends:—

"Aristotle, when he speaks of tragedy, says that the hero ought first to be represented as living in the greatest happiness and splendour. Thus we see him in 'Egmont.' When he is in the enjoyment of felicity, Fate comes and throws a noose over his head from which he is not able to extricate himself. Courage and Defiance appear upon the scene, and boldly look Destiny—aye, and death—in the face. Clärchen's fate interests us, like that of Gretchen in 'Faust,' because she was once so happy. A tragedy which begins as well as continues gloomily, is tedious."

"Leonora" No. 2 was condemned on account of the predominance of the wind instruments, and No. 3 ultimately, because the stringed instruments had so much to do that precision was out of the question.

When, at length, the composer was satisfied with his creation; when the singers (pacified by the friendly intervention of Seyfried, had agreed to give the music as it was written; when all difficulties were apparently overcome, the unlucky composer's annoyances reached a climax in the reception accorded to his work by the public.

With great want of judgment (purposely to annoy him, as Beethoven thought) the opera was produced a few days after the French troops had entered Vienna; when all his friends and patrons, including Lichnowski, had sought refuge at their country seats till the storm had blown over; and the theatre was filled with French officers and soldiers, an audience utterly incapable of appreciating the master. As might have been anticipated, the work was coldly received, and, after three representations, withdrawn. In 1806 it met with the same fate, and not till 1814 did this, the grandest work of the German school—a work which has fought its way to every stage in Europe, and has been brought home to every heart by a Malibran, a Schröder-Devrient, or a Tietjens,—obtain a favourable hearing.

During the time the opera was in progress, Beethoven (like Mozart in producing his "Seraglio") suffered keenly from the jealousy of some of his opponents, and his brothers took care that every barb should find its way home to his sensitive mind. Even his friend Stephan Breuning, in his great desire to help the composer, aggravated the evil by the very warmth of his partisanship,—and thus, by constant dwelling upon them, many little slights assumed a disproportionate magnitude, and annoyed our poor Beethoven intensely.

But enough of darkness and despondency; life now

begins, by one of those sudden and apparently inexplicable changes, to wear a rosier hue for the composer. Reserving our inquiry into the cause of this, we close this chapter with the beautiful letter to the poet Matthison, whose " Adelaïde " he had set to music some time previously.

"MOST ESTEEMED FRIEND,—You will receive, together with this, a composition of mine which has already been printed for several years, but of which, to my shame, you perhaps know nothing yet.

" I may, perhaps, be able to excuse myself, and to explain why I dedicated anything to you, which came so warmly from my heart, and yet did not make you acquainted with it,—by the plea that, at first, I did not know where you resided, and then my diffidence led me to think that I had been somewhat hasty in dedicating anything to you without knowing if it had your approval. And, indeed, even now I send you the 'Adelaïde' with some timidity. You yourself know what changes a few years produce in an artist who is constantly progressing; the more one accomplishes in art, the less is one satisfied with former works.

" My most fervent wish will be realized if you are not altogether dissatisfied with the music to your heavenly 'Adelaïde,' and if you are incited by it to compose a similar poem soon, and (should my request not seem too bold) to send it to me forthwith, when I shall put forth all my strength to approach your lovely poetry in merit.

"Consider the dedication as a mark of my esteem and gratitude for the exquisite pleasure which your poetry has always afforded, and will still afford me.

"When playing the 'Adelaïde,' remember sometimes

"Your sincere admirer,

"BEETHOVEN."

CHAPTER VII.

LOVE.

The Fourth Symphony—Julia Guicciardi—Letters to her—To Bettina Brentano—Beethoven's Attachments—Domestic Troubles—Frau Nanette Streicher—Daily Life—Composing *im Freien*.

> "In love with an Ideal,
> A creature of his own imagination,
> A child of air, and echo of his heart;
> And like a lily on a river floating,
> She floats upon the river of his thoughts."

WHENCE comes it that after a storm of darkness and gloom—after the disappointment of his "Leonora"—the next offspring of the poet's fancy should be a symphony (No. 4), the most delicately finished and bright in colouring which we possess?

The mystery is not easily solved. Former biographers have at once come to the conclusion that this was the period in which Beethoven's love for Julia Guicciardi, alluded to in a letter to Wegeler, had reached its climax. This hypothesis has, however, been put to flight by the discovery of Alexander Thayer that the lady was married to Count Gallenberg (afterwards the Keeper of the Archives of the Imperial Opera) in 1801—that is, five years before the publication of the work.

Is the B flat major Symphony, after all, as much the exponent of the master passion as is, in another way, the C sharp minor Sonata? Or is it, with its troubled, gloomy opening, expanding into glorious warmth and sunshine, another evidence of Beethoven's resolution to set fate at defiance, and to keep at bay the monster Grief which threatened to annihilate him? Who can tell? When the traveller, suddenly emerging from some mist-hung mountain gorge, steps out upon the rocky platform, he beholds in the distance, beneath his delighted gaze, a landscape bathed in sunshine; so to the poet's excited fancy there must have been present some bright vision, one of those "loftier spirits, who sported with him and allotted to him nobler tasks," drawing a veil over the troubled Past, and pointing him onwards to a glorious Future.

Let the Reader take which interpretation he will.

We propose briefly to present to him the two sets of letters which show us Beethoven in two different aspects as a lover—the first *pur et simple*, the second Platonic.

But little is known of the lady, Beethoven's "immortal beloved," whose name vibrates throughout the Adagio of the Moonlight Sonata. The letters to her (written in the year 1800 from some baths in

Hungary, whither he had been ordered for his health) breathe the very intensity of passion—a passion at times too deep for words.*

"*Morning, 6th July.*

"My Angel! my All! my Second Self!

"Only a few words to-day, written with a pencil (with thine). My residence will not be definitely fixed before tomorrow. What a ruinous waste of time!—Why this deep sorrow where Necessity speaks? can our love exist otherwise than by sacrifices, than by our not expecting everything? Canst thou alter the fact that thou art not wholly mine, that I am not wholly thine?—Alas! look into the beauties of Nature, and calm thy mind for what must be endured. Love demands all, and with perfect right, and thus *I feel towards thee* and *thou towards me*, only thou forgettest so easily that I have to live *for myself* and *for thee*,—were we perfectly united, thou wouldst feel this trial as little as I do.

"My journey was terrible. I only arrived yesterday at four o'clock in the morning, owing to the want of horses. The driver chose another route, but what a fearful one! At the last station they warned me not to travel by night, and tried to terrify me by a forest, but this only stimulated me, though I was wrong. The carriage broke down on that dreadful road, a mere rough, unmade country lane, and had not my postillions been what they were, I should have been obliged to remain there by the wayside.

"Esterhazy, on the usual route, had the same fate with eight horses that I had with four, and yet I felt a certain

* In translating these letters we have thought it best to keep to the original pronoun,—the simple *thou* being more suited to Beethoven's ideal love than the coarser *you*.

degree of pleasure, as I always do when I overcome anything happily.—Now, in haste, from the outer to the inner man! We shall probably soon see each other again. I cannot communicate to thee to-day the reflections I have been making, during the last few days, on my life—were our hearts ever near to one another, I should make none such. My heart is full of much that I have to say to thee. Ah! there are moments in which I feel that language is absolutely nothing. Take courage! continue to be my true, my only treasure, my All, as I am thine. The gods must send the rest—that which is ordained to be, and shall be for us.

" Thy faithful
" LUDWIG."

" *Monday evening, 6th July.*

" Thou grievest—thou—the dearest of all beings!—I have just learned that the letters must be sent off very early. Mondays and Thursdays are the only days on which the post goes to K——.—Thou grievest! Ah! where I am, there thou art with me—with our united efforts I shall attain my object—I shall pass my life with thee—what a life!!! whereas now!!! without thee—persecuted at times by the kindness of others, a kindness which I neither deserve nor wish to deserve. Servility from man to his fellow-creature pains me; and, when I consider myself in relation to the universe, what am I? what is he who is called the greatest? and yet even here is displayed the Divine in man!—I weep when I think that thou wilt probably receive no tidings of me before Saturday. However much thou mayest love me, I love thee more fervently still —never hide thy feelings from me.—Good night! as a patient here I must now go to rest. Ah, God! so near!—

so far apart! is not our love a true celestial mansion, enduring as the vault of heaven itself!"

———

"*7th July.*

"Good morning!

"Even before I rise my thoughts throng to thee, my immortal beloved, at times with joy, then again mournfully, waiting to hear if fate be favourable to us. I can only live entirely with thee, or not at all. Yes! I am resolved to wander apart from thee until the moment shall arrive when I may fly into thine arms, may feel my home in thee, and send my soul encompassed by thine into the world of spirits. Yes, alas! it must be so! Thou wilt be prepared, for thou knowest my faithfulness. Never can another possess my heart; never, never. Oh God! why must I fly from what is so dear to me?—and yet my life in V—— is, as at present, a sorrowful one. Thy love made me at once the happiest and the most miserable of men. At my age I require a uniformity, an evenness of life; and can this be possible in our relations?—Angel! I have just heard that the post goes out every day; and must stop that thou mayest receive this letter soon.—Be calm; only by calmly viewing our existence can we attain our aim of passing our lives together. Be calm; love me—to-day—yesterday— what longing, what tears for thee—for thee—for thee—my Life! my All! Farewell! Oh! continue to love me—never misjudge the faithful heart of thy lover. L.

"Ever thine,
"Ever mine,
"Ever each other's."

It was indeed the case that no other love ever did "possess his heart" in the same way. Julia was, if not his first, at least his only *real* love. Such letters as these Beethoven wrote to no one else; the contrast between them and the three following (addressed to Bettina Brentano, afterwards Madame von Arnim) will be at once apparent:—

"*Vienna, August* 11, 1810.

"DEAREST FRIEND,—Never has there been a more beautiful spring than this year; I say so, and feel it too, because in it I first made your acquaintance. You have yourself seen that in society I am like a fish on the sand, which writhes, and writhes, and cannot get off until some benevolent Galatea throws it back into the mighty ocean. I was, indeed, quite out of my element, dearest friend, and was surprised by you at a time when discouragement had completely mastered me—but how quickly it vanished at your glance! I knew at once that you must be from some other sphere than this absurd world, in which, with the best will, one cannot open one's ears. I am a miserable being, and yet I complain of others!!—But you will forgive me for this with that good heart which looks out of your eyes, and that intelligence which is hidden in your ears,—at least they know how to flatter by the way in which they listen.

"My ears are, alas! a partition wall through which I cannot easily have any friendly intercourse with men. Otherwise!—perhaps!—I should have felt more assured with you; but I could only understand the full, intelligent glance of your eyes, which has so taken hold of me, that I shall never forget it. Dear friend, dearest girl!—Art! who understands her? with whom can I discuss this great goddess? . . . How dear to me are the few days in which we chatted together, or, I should say, rather corresponded! I have preserved all the little notes with your witty, charming, most charming answers, and so I have to thank my defective hearing that the best part of those hasty conversations is written down. Since you left I have had vexatious hours,—hours of shadow in which I can do nothing. I wandered in the Schönbrunn Allée for about three hours after you left, but no angel met me who could have taken possession of me as you did, *my Angel.*

"Pardon, dearest friend, this deviation from the original key, but such intervals I must have as a relief to my heart. So you have written about me to Goethe, have you not? I could bury my head in a sack, so that I might not hear or see anything of all that is going on in the world, because I shall not meet you again, dearest angel, but I shall receive a letter from you soon. Hope sustains me, as she does half the world; through all my life she has been my companion. What would otherwise have become of me?—I send you 'Kennst du das Land,' written with my own hand, as a remembrance of the hour in which I first knew you. I send you also another, which I have composed since I took leave of you, my dearest *Herz!*"

> Herz, mein Herz, was soll das geben,
> Was bedränget dich so sehr;
> Welch ein neues, fremdes Leben,
> Ich erkenne dich nicht mehr.

"Answer me at once, dearest friend; write and tell me what is to become of me since my heart has turned such a rebel. Write to your most faithful friend,

"BEETHOVEN."

"*Vienna, 10th February,* 1811.

"Dear, beloved Friend,—I have already had two letters from you, and see from those to Tonie that you still remember me, and even too kindly. Your first letter I carried about with me the whole summer, and it has often made me very happy. Although I do not write to you frequently, and you see nothing at all of me, yet in thought I write you a thousand times a thousand letters. How you must feel in Berlin amongst all the frivolous, worldly rabble, I could imagine, even though you had not written it to me yourself,—mere prating about Art without any results!! The best description of this is to be found in Schiller's poem, 'The River,' in which the Spree speaks.—You are about to be married, dear friend, or are so already, and I have not been able to see you even once previously. May all the felicity with which marriage blesses those who enter into her bonds be poured upon you and your husband! What shall I say to you about myself? I can only exclaim with Johanna, 'Compassionate my fate!' If I am but spared for a few years longer, I will thank Him who embraces all within Himself—the Most High—for this as well as for all other weal and woe.—If you should mention me when writing to Goethe, strive to find all those words which can express to him my deepest reverence and admiration. I am just about to write to him myself regarding 'Egmont,' to which I have composed the music, solely out of love for his poetry, which always makes me happy ;—but who can sufficiently thank a Poet, the most precious jewel of a Nation! Now no more, my dear, good friend. I only returned this morning from a *Bacchanale* where I laughed too heartily, only to weep nearly as much to-day; boisterous joy often drives me violently back upon myself. As to Clemens, many thanks for his courtesy; with regard to the Cantata, the subject is not important enough for us, it is very different in Berlin. As for my affection, the sister has so large a share of it that not much is left for the brother—will he be content with this? Now farewell, dear, dear friend. I imprint a sorrowful kiss upon your forehead, thus impressing, as with a seal, all my thoughts upon it. Write soon, soon, often, to your Brother,

"BEETHOVEN."

"*Toeplitz*, 15*th August*, 1812.

"MY MOST DEAR, KIND FRIEND,—Kings and princes may indeed be able to create professors and privy councillors, and to bestow titles and decorations, but great men they cannot make. Spirits that tower above the common herd, these they cannot pretend to make, and therefore they are forced to respect them. When two men like Goethe and myself come together, these grandees must perceive what is accounted great by such as we.

"On our way home yesterday we met the whole imperial family; we saw them coming in the distance, when Goethe immediately dropped my arm to place himself on one side; and say what I would, I could not get him to advance another step. I pressed my hat down upon my head, buttoned up my great-coat, and made my way with folded arms through the thickest of the throng. Princes and courtiers formed a line, Duke Rudolph took off his hat, the Empress made the first salutation. The great ones of the earth *know me!* To my infinite amusement, I saw the procession file past Goethe, who stood by the side, hat in hand, bending low. I took him to task for it pretty smartly, gave him no quarter, and reproached him with all his sins, especially those against you, dearest friend, for we had just been speaking about you. Heavens! had I been granted a time with you such as *he* had, I should have produced many more great works! A musician is also a poet, and can feel himself transported by a pair of eyes into a more beautiful world, where nobler spirits sport with him, and impose great tasks upon him. What ideas rushed into my mind when I first saw you in the little observatory during that glorious May shower, which proved so fertilizing to me also! The loveliest themes stole from your glances into my heart,—themes which shall enchant the world when Beethoven can no longer direct. If God grant me a few years more, I must see you again, my dearest friend; the voice which ever upholds the right within me demands it. Spirits can also love one another; I shall ever woo yours; your applause is dearer to me than aught else in the world. I told Goethe my opinion of the effect of applause upon men like us—we must be heard with intelligence by our peers; emotion is very well for women (pardon me), but music ought to strike fire from the souls of men. Ah! dearest child, how long is it since we were both so perfectly agreed upon all points! There is no real good but the possession of a pure, good soul, which we perceive in everything, and before which we have no need to dissemble. *We must be something if we would appear something.* The world must recognise us, it is not always unjust; but this is a light matter to me, for I have a loftier aim.

"In Vienna I hope for a letter from you; write soon, soon and fully; in eight days I shall be there. The court goes to-morrow; to-day they are to play once more. Goethe has taught the Empress her *rôle*. His duke and he wished me to play some of my own music, but I refused them both, for they are both in love with Chinese porcelain. A little indulgence is necessary, for understanding seems to have lost the upper hand; but I will not play for such perverse tastes, neither do I choose to be a party to the follies of princes who are for ever committing some such absurdity. Adieu, adieu, dear love; your last letter lay for a whole night next to my heart, and cheered me there. Musicians allow themselves everything. Heavens! how I love you!

"Your most faithful friend and deaf brother,

"BEETHOVEN."

These letters were first published in Bettina's book, "Ilius Pamphilius und die Ambrosia," but the style is so unlike Beethoven's simple mode of expression, that it is difficult to discover what the composer really wrote to Bettina, and what has been supplied by the latter's rather too vivid imagination. The reiterated *dear, dearest,* and the *write soon, soon, often,* are very feminine and very *un-Beethovenish.* This strange, inexplicable little being, who fascinated not only Beethoven, but every one else with whom she came in contact, has also published an account of her interviews with Beethoven. This is so highly coloured that we may be excused for doubting the perfect truth of the recital, especially as we know what a gloss—nay, what falseness—she contrived to give to all that related to her intercourse with Goethe. She herself tells us, naïvely enough, that when she showed Beethoven one morning her account of what he had said the previous day, he was quite surprised, and exclaimed, "Did I really say that? I must have had a *raptus!*"

Bettina was, however, of some service to him, as it was doubtless she who paved the way to his acquaintance with Goethe, and their meeting in 1812 at Toeplitz; and her family remained true, warm friends of the composer long after the great minister had forgotten his very existence.

Beethoven was most unfortunate in his attachments, the objects of which were always of much higher social standing than himself. Constantly associating with people of rank and culture, it was natural that to the sensitive nature of our poet, the young girl nobly born, with all the intuitive, nameless fascinations of the high-bred aristocrat, should present a great contrast to the plebeian, every-day graces of the *bourgeoise*. Beethoven used to say that he had found more real appreciation of his works amongst the nobility than in any other circle, and we can hardly wonder at the infatuation with which he stakes all his chances of happiness on a love which he knows can never be gratified.

The following little scrap in his handwriting has been preserved :—" Only love—yes, only that—has power to give me a happier life. Oh, God! let me at length find her, the one destined to be mine, who shall strengthen me in virtue!" Schindler imagines that these words have reference to a well-known dilettante of great talent, Fräulein Marie Pachler, whom Beethoven admired exceedingly. He never summoned up courage enough to propose to her however, and she afterwards married an advocate in Gratz. This lady may also be the subject of the allusion in a letter to Ries, 1816:—" Say all that is kind from me to your wife; I, alas! have none. I found only one with whom I could have been happy, and she will probably never be mine. But I am not on this account a woman-hater!"

Another love of Beethoven's was the Countess Marie Erdödy, to whom he dedicated the two splendid Trios, Op. 70, but this seems to have been entirely a Platonic affection.

Who can exaggerate the immense benefit that a loving, tender wife would have been to Beethoven—a wife like Mozart's Constance? The consciousness of one ever by his side to whom he might safely confide all that wounded or annoyed him, would have more than neutralized the chilling, exasperating effects of the calamity that had overtaken him, would have been a fresh impetus to great achievements. But fate had willed it otherwise.

In nothing was the want of a wife so apparent as in Beethoven's domestic *ménage*, which certainly was the *non plus ultra* of discomfort. One great cause of this was his habit of frequently changing his abode. He had long since left the Lichnowski Palace, his infirmity rendering it desirable that he should have a home of his own, but he was extremely difficult to please in the choice of a residence. One house he would leave because the sun did not shine into his apartment; another because the supply of water was deficient (a serious drawback to him, as he was accustomed to lave his head and face profusely while composing), and for even less cogent reasons he would pack up and leave at an hour's notice, so that it soon became a difficult matter to find a suitable abode for him. It may easily be imagined that this constant removal was not effected without considerable outlay, and so badly did he manage that at one time he had no less than four houses on his hands. When all other resources failed, he would take refuge in the fourth story of his friend Baron Pasqualati's house, which was constantly reserved for him. The summer he always spent in the country, generally in a hired lodging. On one occasion a suite of apartments in the villa of Baron Pronay had been placed at his disposal, and as the house stood in the midst of a superb park, it was thought that Beethoven would be fully satisfied. In a few days, however, the bird had flown, alleging as his reason that he could not endure to listen to the ceremonious salutation with which his host accosted him every morning in his ramble—much less to return it!

Oulibischeff's amusing description of our composer's surroundings is worth repeating :—

"In his room reigned a confusion, an organized chaos, such as can hardly be imagined. Books and music lay on every article of furniture, or were heaped up like pyramids in the four corners. A multitude of letters which he had received during the week or the month covered the floor like a white carpet with red spots. On the window-sill were displayed the remains of a succulent breakfast, by the side or on the top of proof sheets awaiting correction. There a row of bottles, partly sealed, partly empty; further on an *escritoire*, and on it the sketch of a quartet; on the pianoforte a flying sheet of note-paper with the embryo of a symphony; while to bring so many directly opposite things into harmony, everything was united by a thick layer of dust.

"It may easily be imagined that amidst such a *well-arranged whole*, the artist had often no small trouble to find what he required. He used to complain bitterly about this, and always put the blame on other people's shoulders, for he fancied that he was extremely systematic in the way in which he kept his things, and used to declare that in the darkest night he could find even a pin belonging to him, if people 'would but put things back in their proper places'!

"On one occasion an important paper was missing —neither a sketch nor a loose sheet, but a thick, clearly copied score from the Mass in D. At last it was found; but where, think you? In the kitchen, where it had been used to wrap up eatables! More than one *Donnerwetter!* and more than one bad egg must have flown at the head of the devoted cook, when this was discovered; for Beethoven liked fresh eggs too well to use them as missiles. . . . Once, when he had dismissed his housekeeper, a very good orderly person (and soon received into favour again), he resolved to make himself independent, and to keep no more servants, since they only 'worked mischief in the house.' And why should he not wait upon himself, and look after the kitchen himself? Could it be more difficult to prepare a dinner than to prepare a C minor symphony? Charmed with this glorious idea, Beethoven hastens to put it into execution. He invites some friends to dinner, buys the necessary provisions in the market, and carries them home himself; ties on the business-like white apron; adjusts the indispensable nightcap on his head; grasps the cook's knife, and sets to work. The guests arrive, and find him before the fire, whose scorching flame seems to act like the fire of inspiration upon him. The patience of the Viennese appetites was put to an unwonted trial. At length the dishes were placed on the table, and the host proved that it was worth while waiting for him. The soup might have challenged the *soupe maigre* given in charity; the boiled meat, scarcely cooked, presupposed in individuals of the human race the digestion of an ostrich; the vegetables swam in a sea of fat and water; the roast meat, splendidly burned to a cinder, looked as though it had found its way down the chimney; in short, nothing was fit to eat. And nobody did eat anything except the host, who by word and example encouraged his guests to fall to. In vain; Beethoven's *chefs-d'œuvre* of cookery were not appreciated, and the guests made their dinner on bread, fruit, and sweetmeats, adding plenty of wine to prevent any bad effects from their enforced abstinence. This remarkable feast convinced even the great Maestro that composing and cooking are two very different things, and the unjustly deposed cook was speedily re-established in her rights."

It was very fortunate for Beethoven that after some years passed in this erratic way, a sensible lady-friend at length came to the rescue, and by her feminine tact and adroitness, succeeded in persuading him to abandon his nomadic habits to some extent, and to mingle a little more in society. This was Frau Nanette Streicher, the amiable wife of the celebrated instrument maker, and early friend of Schiller. She began by putting the wardrobe of the composer to rights (as might be imagined, it was in a deplorable plight), and afterwards, in conjunction with her husband, hired a respectable house for Beethoven, furnished it suitably, and engaged a man (a tailor by trade) and his wife to wait upon him. In this quiet haven our tempest-tossed Beethoven came to anchor for a while, and might have been seen busy over his pianoforte, or among his papers, while his cross-legged knight of the Goose stitched away comfortably in the adjoining anteroom.

When fairly domiciled, Beethoven's mode of life was very regular. His habit was to rise every morning, winter and summer, at daybreak, when he at once proceeded to his desk, where he wrote till about two o'clock without any interruption, except the necessary interval for breakfast, and—if his ideas did not flow rapidly enough—an occasional run of half an hour or longer into the open air. Between two and three he dined, after which it was his invariable custom to make the circuit of the town twice or three times; and no weather could keep him within doors—summer heat or winter frost, thunder, hail, rain, sleet,—nothing prevented this afternoon ramble. It was, in fact, his time for composition; he never ventured out without his note-book to preserve any fugitive thoughts that might flit across his mind, and used laughingly to apply to himself Johanna's words, "I dare not come without my banner!" Necessarily, therefore, he was a very silent companion, but in *one* sense only, as the whole way he continued humming (or rather growling) in a manner peculiar to himself any thema on which he was mentally at work. Ries relates that on one occasion when they were walking together, Beethoven suddenly exclaimed, "A theme has occurred to me!" They hurried onwards in silence, and on arriving at home the master went at once to the pianoforte (without even removing his hat), where he thundered like an inspired giant for more than an hour, during which the beautiful finale to the Sonata Op. 57 (Appassionata) struggled into existence.

Beethoven generally returned from his promenade only when warned by the shadows that evening was coming on; then alone in the darkening twilight he loved to breathe to his best, his only friend, his *clavier*,* the thoughts which met with no response in human sympathy. During the evening he very seldom worked, but would smoke his pipe, and play occasionally on his viola or violin, both of which

---

* Beethoven could not endure the foreign word *pianoforte*.

must always be placed ready for him on the pianoforte.

Our poor deaf Beethoven had, too, his little coterie of sincere and attached friends, among whom his real nature could show itself without restraint or distrust, and who clung to him through life in spite of the unceasing efforts of the two brothers to dislodge them. These were—naturally Prince Lichnowski and his brother Count Moritz, who cherished a love and admiration for Beethoven which the latter warmly reciprocated, dedicating to the Count his Variations, Op. 35, and the beautiful Idyl, Op. 90. To these must be added the comical little Baron von Zmeskall, a Hungarian State Secretary, to whom the composer addressed many a humorous epistle; his old friend Stephan Breuning; the Baron von Gleichenstein; his secretary Schindler; and last, but not least, Franz, Count von Brunswick, to whom he dedicated the Sonata Appassionata, and who had more influence over him than anybody else.

One proceeding Beethoven never omitted, viz., the reading of the evening paper. In these stirring times the newspaper was an absolute necessity, and our musician would never retire to rest without previously ascertaining the state of the political horizon. He used to frequent a coffee-house which boasted another means of exit besides the general one, and taking up his position in the background, he would steadily peruse the *Gazette* (not a very long task in those days, when "our own" correspondents were as yet undreamt of), and as soon as the last word of the last page had been scanned, beat a hasty retreat through the private door, and wend his solitary way homewards. Ten o'clock rarely found him out of bed. Such was his simple, innocent day! It was no mere phrase, that declaration of his, "*I live only in my art*,"—it was indeed the one connecting link between him and others.

What he produced in suffering and loneliness stirred, like a mighty wind among the forest branches, the noblest feelings of a thousand hearts, bidding them grapple with Destiny as he had done, and prove themselves *men* and heroes!

CHAPTER VIII.

VICTORY AND SHADOW.

Period of Greatest Intellectual Activity—Hummel—The Battle of Vittoria—Congress of Vienna—Maelzel—Pecuniary Difficulties—Adoption of Nephew—The Philharmonic Society—The Classical and Romantic Schools—The Ninth Symphony—His Nephew's Conduct—Last Illness.

THE period between the years 1805 and 1814 may be considered that of Beethoven's greatest creative energy. It is almost impossible to keep pace with the stream of colossal works which flowed without intermission from his pen. To this period belong the G major and E flat pianoforte concertos, without exception the most poetical and the noblest compositions of the kind which we possess; the fantasia for pianoforte, orchestra, and chorus; the fourth, fifth, sixth, seventh, and eighth symphonies; the " Calm Sea and Prosperous Voyage" on Goethe's short but suggestive poem, "*Tiefe Stille herrscht im Wasser; ohne Regung ruht das Meer;*" the First Mass; the music to "Egmont;" the overtures to Collin's tragedy of "Coriolanus," and to "King Stephen," and the "Ruins of Athens,"—each of which, from its intellectual grasp of subject, wonderful ideality, and highly finished detail, would merit a volume to itself. Nor do these Titanic orchestral productions occupy the whole of his attention. They are accompanied by a mass of works for the pianoforte, which, if in one sense slighter than those we have named, yet, in another, stand equally high; the soliloquies and dialogues (if we may be allowed the expression) contained in the pianoforte sonatas breathe thoughts as noble and as deep as those expressed by the more varied *dramatis personæ* of the orchestra or the quartets. Truly, a perfect acquaintance with Beethoven would claim the devotion of the highest powers, and the study of a lifetime. Any attempt, however, to depict these great works briefly in words would be futile, and we therefore pass on to the consideration of the poet's outer life. This was almost monotonous—certainly not varied. Beethoven, as we have seen, lived wholly in his art, and the changes which occurred, most momentous to him, were not those of outward circumstance, but of inner, intellectual development.

In the year 1809 he was offered the post of Kapellmeister to the King of Westphalia, with a salary of six hundred ducats; and this, his great desire of possessing a fixed income made him ready to accept; although he would certainly have been miserable in such a position, as Jerome was not the man to understand either him or his works. Happily, this ordeal was spared him. It was thought derogatory to the dignity of Austria that her greatest composer, the one of whom she had most reason to be proud, should be allowed through pecuniary considerations to quit her bounds ; and as the Emperor would do nothing for Beethoven (his abhorrence of etiquette and well-known republican sentiments having prevented his ever getting into favour at Court), an agreement was ultimately entered into by the Archduke Rudolph (Beethoven's pupil, afterwards Archbishop of Olmütz) and the Princes Lobkowitz and Kinsky, to pay the composer annually the sum of four thousand guldens, on condition of his continuing to reside in Vienna. In two years' time this was reduced one-fifth, owing to changes in the Austrian Finance, and subsequently it dwindled down to a mere nothing, from the death and bankruptcy of two of the contracting parties—but Beethoven could get no redress, although he religiously fulfilled his part of the compact.

In drawing the money from the executors of Prince Kinsky he was obliged always to send in a proof that he was still in existence. This annoyed him excessively, and he generally had the affair transacted for him by a friend, which on one occasion produced the following laconic voucher to Schindler :—

"CERTIFICATE OF LIFE.—The Fish lives! *vidi* Pastor Romualdus,"—an allusion to his eccentric use of water when composing.

In this year also occurred the bombardment of

Vienna, out of which Ries has contrived to bring forward an implied accusation of cowardice against the composer, in his statement that Beethoven hid himself in a cellar, burying his head among cushions that he might not hear the firing.

The explanation of this lies on the surface; if he did take refuge underground it was only what every other inhabitant of the city, whose duty did not call him elsewhere, was doing; and as for the cushions— the vibration of the cannonade heard in that vault must have been agony to his diseased nerve. Had Beethoven really been alarmed he might easily have quitted Vienna. Cowardice in any form is the last vice that could be attributed to him; resolute and firm, he feared no danger.

In 1810 the Mass in C was performed for the first time at Eisenstadt, the residence of Prince Esterhazy, the grandson of Haydn's patron, in whose service Hummel was at the time as Kapellmeister. Esterhazy, accustomed only to the simple services and masses of the Haydn-Mozart school, did not know what to make of a production so totally different. Accordingly, at the *déjeuner* afterwards given in the palace to the artists and dilettanti who had assembled for the occasion, he said, with a smile, to our composer, "Now, dear Beethoven, what is this that you have been about again?" The susceptible musician, not a little irritated at hearing his work so lightly spoken of, glanced towards Hummel, who happened to be standing by the Prince's side, wearing a peculiar smile, which seemed to Beethoven full of malicious pleasure. This was too much—the opinion of a fashionable worldling like Esterhazy was nothing to Beethoven, but that a brother in art should so misunderstand him—should rejoice at an -apparent failure!—he rose abruptly, and quitted the palace.

Such is the correct account of the rupture between Beethoven and Hummel, which lasted until a few days before the death of the former, when Hummel, hearing of his precarious state, hastened to Vienna to effect a reconciliation before it was too late.* Another version of the story is that the two composers were rivals for the hand of the same lady, and that Hummel, owing to Beethoven's deafness and his own better position as Kapellmeister, was the favoured suitor! The practice of tracing every event in our composer's life to a love affair is just as ridiculous as the opposite extreme of denying his capability for the tender passion.

A more interesting incident in connection with the First Mass is that related by Schindler of the effect produced upon Beethoven by the reading of the German text composed for it by some poet, who, though unknown to fame, seems to have translated the master's thoughts from the language of Tones into that of Words, with power and truth. When

---

* While this little volume was going through the press, Dr. Ferdinand Hiller kindly offered to send us for insertion an account of those last interviews between the two great composers, of which he was himself an eye-witness, being at the time a pupil of Hummel, whom he accompanied to Beethoven's residence. Unfortunately, the offer arrived too late.

Beethoven came to the "*Qui tollis*" his eyes overflowed with tears (the first and last time that he was ever seen so affected) as he exclaimed, "Thus I felt while composing this!"

The tide of Beethoven's earthly renown and glory, which had been slowly rising for years, reached its height in 1813-14.

In the former year took place the two celebrated concerts on behalf of the Austrian and Bavarian soldiers wounded in the battle of Hanau, when the Seventh Symphony, and "Wellington's Victory, or the Battle of Vittoria," were performed for the first time. We can easily imagine, from the sensation excited even now by the latter work, how intense must have been the enthusiasm which greeted its performance at a time when popular feeling was strung up to the highest pitch. Beethoven himself directed, regulating the movements of his bâton by those of Schuppanzigh's bow. In a notice of the concert written by himself he says: "It was an unprecedented assembly of distinguished artists, every one of whom was inspired by the desire of accomplishing something by his art for the benefit of the Fatherland; and all worked together unanimously, accepting of subordinate places without regard to precedence, that a splendid *ensemble* might be attained. . . . My part was the direction of the whole, but only because the music happened to be of my composition. Had it been otherwise, I would have stationed myself as readily at the great drum, like Herr Hummel; for our only motives were Love to the Fatherland, and the joyful devotion of our powers to serve those who had sacrificed so much for us."

In 1814 occurred the great Congress, when Vienna was for a season the abode of kings, princes, and delegates from every Court in Europe, and the glittering capital was well-nigh intoxicated by its own magnificence. The magistrates of the city invited Beethoven to compose a Cantata for the occasion, which produced the "Glorreiche Augenblick," perhaps the composer's most neglected work, and deservedly so, as it is not worthy of him. It won for him, however, the presentation of the freedom of the city, the only distinction which Beethoven valued. Nor was this his only triumph. His genius began to be universally recognised; he was created an honorary member of Academies and Societies in London, Paris, Stockholm, and Amsterdam; and the Philharmonic Society in London presented him with a superb grand pianoforte of Broadwood's manufacture. In short, from every nation in Europe, and even from America, he received striking proofs of the love and admiration in which he was held. Stimulated by these manifestations, excited by the splendour around him, and the stirring, momentous events which were taking place, Beethoven was induced to depart for the time from his usual solitary habits, and to mingle for a few weeks in society. In the apartments of Prince Rasoumowski, the well-known Russian dilettante, he was introduced to many of the illustrious visitors, and long retained a lively recollection, half comical, half gratified, of the manner in which he had been idolized;—how the grand seigneurs had paid court to him, and how admirably he had played his part in receiving their homage! He was most deeply affected by his interview with the gentle Empress Elizabeth of Russia, with whom he conversed in his customary frank, open way, completely setting aside all etiquette; while she, on her part, expressed the highest veneration for the composer, and at her departure left him a gift of two hundred ducats, which he acknowledged after his own fashion by dedicating to her his brilliant Polonaise, Op. 89. This was the only substantial result to our poverty-stricken Beethoven of the attachment professed by the whole of the gay throng!

The bright episode of the Congress, with its fêtes and triumphs, soon flitted past, bringing out in sterner and darker contrast the days which followed.

Beethoven had dedicated his "Battle of Vittoria" to the Prince Regent of England (George IV.), but to his great chagrin, no notice was taken of it. He alludes to this in a letter to Ries, and referring to the Prince's well-known character of *gourmand*, says, "He might at least have sent me a butcher's knife or a turtle!"

Another vexation in connection with the symphony, causing him infinite annoyance, arose out of the despicable conduct of Maelzel, afterwards the inventor of the metronome. In the year 1812 he had made the acquaintance of the latter, who had promised to construct for him a sound-conductor, in return for which Beethoven composed a kind of warlike piece for the mechanician's new instrument, the panharmonica, which he was on the point of taking to England for exhibition. The effect of Beethoven's work was so marvellous, that Maelzel urged him to arrange it for the orchestra, and the result was—the "Battle of Vittoria." Maelzel meanwhile went on constructing four machines, only one of which was found available, and Beethoven, without the slightest suspicion of any underhand dealing, allowed him to take the entire management of the concerts for the relief of the wounded. In his hermit life he did not hear much of what was going on around him, and his consternation may therefore be imagined when informed that his false friend was announcing the symphony everywhere as his own property, stating that it had been given to him by Beethoven in return for his machine, and the sum of four hundred guldens which he professed to have lent him! He had actually contrived to have many of the orchestral parts copied out, and those that were wanting supplied by some low musician, and with this mutilated work he was on his way to England. The matter was at once placed in the hands of the law; but it was long before Beethoven recovered from the effects of this fraud; it made him, in fact, suspicious ever after towards copyists. The loan of four hundred guldens proved to have been *fifty*, which Beethoven accepted from him at a time when, as he states in his instructions to his lawyers, he was "in dire necessity; *deserted by every one in Vienna.*"

This Maelzel had the impudence subsequently to

write to Beethoven, requesting his patronage for the metronome, and pretending that he was busily engaged in preparing a sound-conductor which would enable the master to direct in the orchestra. The latter never made its appearance, but Beethoven, who at first approved of the metronome, did all in his power to have it introduced. Afterwards, when he saw the confusion of *tempo* which it had occasioned, he used to say, "Don't let us have any metronome! He that has true feeling will not require it, and for him who has none, it will not be of any use."

This affair with Maelzel gives us a glimpse into the pecuniary difficulties which harassed Beethoven throughout his life, assuming greater prominence towards the end. He was always in want of money, and yet (according to the notions of the times) he was handsomely paid for his compositions. What, then, was the cause of it? Were his means swallowed up by his frequent removals? Did the perplexity arise simply from his unbusiness-like habits? To these questions we must add a third, which may, perhaps, afford a clue to the mystery,—What became of the valuable presents, the watches, rings, breast-pins, snuff-boxes, &c., &c., of which Beethoven had received so many? When asked where such a gift was, he would look bewildered, and say after a moment's reflection, "I really don't know!" The matter would then pass entirely from his thoughts; but there were those about him who were not equally indifferent!

In 1815 the cloud which for two years had been threatening, burst upon him in those troubles and sorrows which encompassed him until the end. He lost his old friend and staunch supporter, Prince Lichnowski, and, a few months, after his brother Carl, who in dying bequeathed to him as a legacy the care of his only child. It seemed as if the annoyance which this man had caused our Beethoven in his life were to be perpetuated and continually renewed in the person of his son. Not so, however, did the master regard the fresh call upon him. After having done all that kindness could suggest, or money procure, to relieve his brother's sufferings and cheer his last days, he took home the orphan child to his heart with a love and tenderness that could not have been greater had the boy been his own.

His first step was to remove him from the care of his mother, a woman of lax morals and low habits. In this Beethoven was actuated by the purest and best motives; but, unfortunately, his zeal went too far. He forgot that the fact of his sister-in-law's having been a bad wife did not necessarily imply that she had lost a mother's heart; and in insisting upon the total separation between the two, he roused all the bitterest feelings of a woman's nature, and prepared much sorrow for himself. The "Queen of Night," as he nicknamed her, sought redress through the law, and for four years a suit for the possession of the lad was pending. In his appeal Beethoven thus nobly expresses the sentiments which dictated his conduct:—" My wishes and efforts have no other aim than that of giving the best possible education to the boy, his talents justifying the greatest expectations; and of fulfilling the trust reposed in my brotherly love by his father. The stem is now pliable; but if it be for a time neglected, it will become crooked, and outgrow the gardener's training hand; and upright bearing, knowledge, and character will be irretrievably lost. I know of no duty more sacred than that of the training and education of a child. The duty of a guardian can only consist in the appreciation of what is good, and the adoption of a right course; and only then does he consult the welfare of his ward; whereas in obstructing the good he neglects his duty."

Misled by the prefix *van*, his advocate unfortunately carried the case to the Aristocratic Court; and, as it went on, Beethoven was called upon to show his right to this proceeding. Pointing with eloquent emphasis to his head and heart, the composer declared that in these lay his nobility; but, however true in the abstract, the law could not admit this plea, and after a decision had been given in his favour, the case had to be re-tried before the ordinary Civil Court. This occurrence wounded Beethoven more than can be described; he felt his honour tarnished as a man and as an artist, and for several months no persuasion could induce him to show himself in public. In addition to this, the evidence necessarily brought forward to strengthen his plea revealed only too plainly the loose life of his sister-in-law, and such an *exposé* of one so nearly related to himself was, for his pure and reserved nature, the height of misery.

The Civil Court reversed the decision of the Aristocratic, and the boy was given over to his mother; while Beethoven, determined to gain his end, brought the case before the High Court of Appeal, where he was finally successful. Let the reader imagine the effect of all this painful publicity, following upon the annoyances with Maelzel, to a mind constituted like Beethoven's. No Stylites on his pillar could have suffered more than did our composer in his loneliness until the cause was gained. And what return did he meet with from the object of his solicitude?—The basest ingratitude.

About this time he began seriously to think of visiting London; the Philharmonic Society made him the most handsome offers; and his own inclinations prompted him to quit Vienna. He had at all times cherished the greatest love and admiration for England and the English nation, our free institutions harmonizing with his political views; and a commission coming from this quarter was always welcome to him, not only on account of the unwonted *honoraire* which usually accompanied it, but also because of the high esteem in which he held the English as artists and appreciators of art. During the latter years of his life, therefore, this visit to London was his favourite scheme, and he intended *en route* to pass through the Rhine provinces, that he might once more see the home and the friends of his boyhood;—but it was destined never to take place.

The four years of the lawsuit were almost barren of creative result, but in the winter of 1819-20 he began his Mass in D. This colossal work, written more for future generations than for us, was originally intended for the installation of the Archduke Rudolph as Archbishop of Olmütz; but as the work went on, our composer grew more and more in love with his task, which gradually assumed such proportions that it was not completed till 1823—two years after the event it was meant to celebrate! A copy of the Mass, which Beethoven regarded as his most successful effort, was offered to every court in Europe for the sum of fifty ducats. It was, however, accepted only by France, Prussia, Saxony, Russia, and by Prince Radziwill, Governor of Posen, and a musical society in Frankfort. The King of Prussia sent to inquire, through his Ambassador, if the master would not prefer a decoration to the fifty ducats. Beethoven's answer was prompt—" Fifty ducats !" If his work were worthy of a decoration, why not have given it in addition to the paltry sum asked for it? Louis XVIII. acted differently; he sent the composer a valuable gold medal, on one side of which was his bust, and on the reverse the inscription, "*Donné, par le roi, à M. Beethoven.*" An application of Beethoven's to Goethe requesting him to draw the attention of Karl August to the Mass met with no answer, although Goethe might have been able, at very trifling inconvenience to himself, to render material assistance to the master. His self-love had probably not recovered from the shock it had received during a walk with Beethoven on the Bastei at Vienna, when, struck by the profound respect and deference manifested by every one whom they encountered, Goethe exclaimed, "I really had no idea that I was so well known here!" "Oh!" replies our brusque composer, "the people are bowing to me, not to you!" This was in reality the case, for the circumstance occurred in Beethoven's palmy days, when he was, as Marx observes, a "universally beloved and popular character, a part of Vienna itself."

The circumstance which more than any other casts a gloom over the master's last days is, that he was doomed (apparently) to outlive his fame, and to have the inexpressible mortification of witnessing that rupture in the musical world which has lasted down to our days, and will probably never be healed, viz., the separation of the classical from the so-called romantic school. Hitherto, the followers of Art had been united ; naturally, individual tastes and predilections had occasionally predominated—some admiring one master and some another,—but on the whole, the lovers of music had been unanimous in their adherence to the pure and good. With the appearance of Rossini (that clever scene-painter, as Beethoven called him), this state of affairs underwent a complete revolution. His gay, light-hearted melodies, extravagant roulades, and inexhaustible vivacity took the public by storm—Beethoven and his immortal masterpieces were forgotten. And yet, perhaps, this is only what might have been expected,— the divine in Art is not for all, nor are all for the divine. Beethoven might have known, like Goethe, that he was too profound ever to be popular in a wide sense. The mass of mankind look upon Art simply as a means of relaxation. So, indeed, it ought to be to all; but never should it stop there. Art, in its highest and best forms, has power not only to provide the weary and careworn with temporary self-forgetfulness, and to dissipate grief, but—and herein lies its true, its God-given strength —to renew the energies and brace the mind for higher and nobler efforts in the future. Whenever it stops short of this, satisfied with fulfilling its first and lower function, there is developed a tendency to abdicate its real position, and to degenerate into the mere panderer to man's follies, to his vices. Who could have felt this more keenly than Beethoven? Not the mere loss of his own popularity was it that made him turn away so deeply wounded from grand displays in which snatches of his own works were performed, along with meaningless arias, and shallow, noisy overtures of the new Italian school. So deeply did he take the change to heart, that he resolved to have his Mass in D and the Ninth Symphony performed for the first time in Berlin. The announcement of this intention produced a warm remonstrance (in the form of an Address) from his attached little circle of friends; and the master, touched by the feeling which called out this manifestation, was induced to forego his determination, and to consent to the two works being brought out in Vienna, provided a hall suitable for the purpose could be obtained.

This was no easy matter, and the difficulties in connection with it gave rise to a half-comical little incident. His enemies were in power, and demanded an absurd sum for the use of the building, to which Beethoven could not be induced to agree. As neither party would yield, the project seemed on the point of shipwreck, when the faithful Schindler, alarmed for the success of the enterprise on which he had set his heart, persuaded Count Moritz Lichnowski and the violinist Schuppanzigh to meet him as if by accident at Beethoven's house, and press the latter to yield to what was inevitable. The plan succeeded, and the necessary papers were signed; but the composer's suspicions were roused, and the three devoted friends received for their pains the following autocratic mandates :—

"To COUNT MORITZ LICHNOWSKI,—

"Duplicity I despise. Visit me no more. There will be no concert. "BEETHOVEN."

"To HERR SCHUPPANZIGH,—

"Come no more to see me. I shall give no concert.
"BEETHOVEN."

"To HERR SCHINDLER,—

"Do not come to me until I send for you. No concert.
"BEETHOVEN."

This did not in the least deter them, however, from doing what they believed necessary for his benefit : the concert took place, and was the scene of a triumph such as few have experienced. The glorious Jupiter Symphony seemed to act upon the immense mass of human beings that thronged the building in every part, like ambrosial nectar; they became intoxicated with delight, and when the refrain was caught up by the choir, "*Seid umschlungen Millionen!*" a shout of exuberant joy rent the air, completely drowning the singers and instruments. But there stood the master in the midst, his face turned towards the orchestra, absorbed and sunk within himself as usual,—he heard nothing, saw nothing. Fräulein Unger, the soprano, turned him gently round, and then what a sight met his astonished gaze,—a multitude transported with joy! Almost all were standing, and the greater number melted to tears, now for the first time realizing fully the extent of Beethoven's calamity.—Probably in all that great assembly the master himself was the most unmoved. Simply bowing in response to the ovation, he left the theatre gloomy and despondent, and took his homeward way in silence.

Verily, he, like a Greater, knew what was in man. In eight days from this eventful epoch he was completely forgotten; a second concert proved an utter failure, and Rossini's star was again in the ascendant. Nor did the flighty Viennese public cast another thought upon our Beethoven until the news of his death came upon them like the shock of an earthquake, and they hastened, when it was too late, to repair the past.

But if it was painful to meet with ingratitude from the public, how much harder must it have been for the master to endure the same from one nearly related to him! We have said that he adopted his brother's orphan child. This nephew, also a Carl Beethoven, was at his father's death about eight years of age, and a boy of great talent and promise. The four succeeding years, during which the lawsuit dragged its weary length, were extremely detrimental to him, as he seems to have been tossed about from one person to another—now with his mother, and again with his uncle—in a manner very prejudicial to any good moral development. Events showed him only too plainly the character of his mother, but nature—stronger still—urged him to take her part in the contest so far as he dared; and, incited by her evil counsels, he soon began secretly to despise his uncle's authority, and openly to follow a path he had laid down for himself,—the path of self-will and sensual indulgence. Expelled from the University where he was attending the Philosophical Course, his more than father received the repentant prodigal with open arms, and placed him in the Polytechnic School to study for a mercantile career, that he might be under the supervision of Herr Reisser, Vice-President of the Institute, and co-guardian with himself over Carl. In the summer of 1825 the composer wrote no fewer than twenty-nine letters to his erring nephew, every one of which exhibits his character in the most beautiful light. They breathe the cry of a David, "Oh! Absalom! my son! my son!"—but it is a living Absalom who has to be lamented, and the most energetic appeals, the most loving remonstrances are invoked to move that stony heart. In vain,—Carl went from bad to worse, and in 1826 the master was compelled to give up the habit which had been his only solace for years—that of spending the summer in the country—and to remain in Vienna to watch over the young man. Matters soon came to a crisis, —Carl, urged to pass an examination which he had long neglected, attempted, in a fit of despair, to put an end to his own life. Here the law stepped in, and after he had been treated in an asylum where his spiritual as well as his bodily condition was cared for, the miserable youth was restored to his no less wretched uncle, with orders to quit Vienna within four-and-twenty hours. Beethoven's old friend, Stephan Breuning, exerted himself to procure a cadetship for the lad, and he was at length permitted to join the regiment of the Baron von Stutterheim, to whom the composer gratefully dedicated one of his last quartets. Pending this arrangement the unhappy uncle and nephew took refuge at Gneixendorf, the estate of Johann v. Beethoven, who had offered them a temporary asylum. A few days here, however, were enough for the composer; irritated by the unjust reproaches and low taunts of his brother, he determined at once to return to Vienna, taking his nephew with him. It was a raw, cold, miserable day in December; Johann refused to lend his close carriage to him to whom he owed all his prosperity, and Beethoven was obliged to perform a long journey in an open conveyance, with no shelter from the keen wind and pitiless rain. His health, which had long been failing, sank under this exposure, and he arrived in Vienna with a severe attack of inflammation of the lungs, which ultimately caused his death.

As soon as they arrived at home, Carl was charged instantly to procure a physician for his uncle, one Dr. Wawruch; but this loving nephew's whole thoughts were for his old companions and his old haunts. He went to play billiards, entrusting his commission to the tender mercies of a servant of the establishment, who, in his turn, let the affair pass entirely from his memory until two days after, when he happened to be taken ill himself, and to be carried *by chance* to the same hospital in which the doctor practised. At the sight of the physician his instructions flashed upon his memory, and he besought him to go at once to the great Beethoven. Horror-struck, Dr. Wawruch, who was an enthusiastic admirer of the composer, hastened to his house and found him lying in the most precarious state, completely alone and neglected. His unwearied efforts so far succeeded that Beethoven rallied for a time, and his first act was—to appoint his worthless nephew sole heir to all his effects! Soon symptoms of dropsy showed themselves, he had to be tapped four times, and it became evident that the master spirit would soon leave its earthly tabernacle for a better and more enduring habitation. He was always resigned and patient, remarking, with a smile, when a painful operation was being performed, "Better water from my body than from my pen!"

The Philharmonic Society sent him a magnificent edition of Handel, and the greatest pleasure of his last days consisted in going through the works of his favourite composer.

His illness, however, lasted some time; in the meanwhile he was making nothing, and his small resources began to fail him. The money he had recently made by his works he had added to the fund which he sacredly kept for his nephew, and which no persuasion could induce him to touch; he had been disappointed in a sum owing to him by the Russian dilettante, Prince Galitzin; and in great distress the question arose, what was he to do? to whom could he turn? He bethought him of the offer made by the Philharmonic Society in London to give a concert for his benefit, and, after much hesitation, finally applied to them, through Moscheles and Sir George Smart, for the fulfilment of the promise. His countrymen have never been able to forgive Beethoven for this step, especially as it was found after his death that he had left about £1,200; but this, as we said before, he looked upon as his nephew's property, and would not appropriate any of it to his own use—therefore, what was he to do? *Forsaken by the whole world in Vienna*, was he to starve? The society rejoiced in the opportunity of showing the gratitude of England to him who has placed the whole human race under an eternal obligation, and immediately despatched £100 to Vienna, with the intimation that if this were not sufficient more would be forthcoming.

Alas! more was not required; a few days after the gift arrived the great musician breathed his last. We leave the description of the closing scene to Schindler:—

"When I went to him on the morning of the 24th of March, 1827, I found him with distorted face, and so weak that only by the greatest effort could he utter a few words. In a short time the physician entered, and, after looking at him in silence, whispered to me that Beethoven was advancing with rapid steps towards dissolution. As we had fortunately provided for the signing of the will some days previously, there remained to us but *one* ardent wish— that of proving to the world that he died as a true Christian. The physician, therefore, wrote a few lines, begging him in the name of all his friends to allow the holy sacrament to be administered to him, upon which he answered calmly and collectedly, 'I will.' The physician then left, that I might arrange for this; and Beethoven said to me, 'I beg you to write to Schott, and send him the document, he will require it; write to him in my name, I am too weak; and tell him that I beg him earnestly to send the wine he promised. If you have time to-day, write also to England.' The pastor came about twelve o'clock, and the holy office was performed with the greatest solemnity.

"Beethoven himself now began to believe in his approaching end; for hardly had the clergyman gone than he exclaimed, '*Plaudite amici, comedia finita est;* have I not always said that it would come thus?' He then begged me again not to forget Schott, and to thank the Philharmonic Society once more for their gift, adding that the society had cheered his last days, and that even on the verge of the grave he thanked them and the whole English nation. At this moment the servant of Herr von Breuning entered with the little case of wine sent by Schott. I placed two bottles of Rudesheimer on the table by his side; he looked at them and said, 'What a pity!—too late!' These were his last words. In a few moments he fell into an agony so intense that he could no longer articulate. Towards evening he lost consciousness, and became delirious. This lasted till the evening of the 25th, when visible signs of death already showed themselves. Notwithstanding, he lingered till the evening of the 26th, when his spirit took flight, while without a violent storm of thunder and lightning seemed to reflect his death struggle in Nature herself—his best friend."

The last agonies of the master were soothed by but *one* friendly touch, that of Anselm Hüttenbrenner from Gratz, who had hurried into Vienna to press the loved hand once more. He was borne to his last resting-place by an immense concourse, exceeding twenty thousand; composers, poets, authors, artists, surrounded his coffin with lighted torches, while the choristers sang to one of his own melodies the words of Grillparzer:—

> "Du, dem nie im Leben,
> Ruhestätt ward, und Heerd und Haus,
> Ruhe nun im stillen
> Grabe, nun im Tode aus,"—

Thou, who ne'er in life hadst resting-place, nor hearth, nor home—rest thee now in the quiet grave—in death. Amen.

THE PIANOFORTE SONATAS.*

FROM Domenico Scarlatti down to Frederic Chopin a succession of cembalists, clavecinists, and pianists rich in talent, art, and genius, have created a series of select works, the counterpart of which, in number, variety, and lasting fame, can probably be displayed by no other branch of musical literature. Two collections, however, take precedence of all this wealth of tone-poetry; these are the Fugues and Preludes (the "Wohl-temperirte Clavier") of Johann Sebastian Bach, and the Sonatas of Ludwig van Beethoven. Both works have been so much discussed, have been analyzed in so many different ways, have had such multifarious constructions put upon them, have been praised and extolled from so many different standpoints, that the conviction must be impressed upon every observer —*they are inexhaustible.* This is really the case—they are an ever-flowing spring of study for the composer and the pianist, and of enjoyment for the educated hearer. At present, however, we have only to do with the Sonatas of Beethoven, and must therefore direct our attention to them.

Most of the German composers have become great at the pianoforte. They learned to command the technicalities

* From an edition of the Sonatas published in Breslau.

of this compendium of sound, song, harmony, and polyphony, and it became to them a voice, a second tongue, a part of themselves. Upon it they could express every whispering musical emotion, and lend words, we may even say, to every passing mood which stirred their sensitive souls; the utterances which Bach, Mozart, and Beethoven confided to their pianoforte in lonely hours may have surpassed in beauty (if not in perfection of form) what they committed to writing. In no other master, however, does this familiar intercourse between the tone-poet and his instrument present itself to our minds with such wondrous clearness as in Beethoven. In his mighty symphonies he speaks to the crowd like an ideal world's orator, raising them to the highest emotions of purified humanity; in his quartets he strives to impart to each instrument an almost dramatic individuality; but in his Pianoforte Sonatas he speaks to himself, or, if you will, to the instrument, as to his dearest friend. He relates his most secret joys and sorrows, his longing and his love, his hope and his despair. An entire, full, real, inner human life is revealed to us—sound, energetic (*kernig*), manly. Whether he gives himself up to passionate outpourings or to melancholy laments, whether he jests, plays, dreams, laughs, or weeps, he continues always simple and true. We find no straining after effect, no oddity, no coquettishness, no sentimentality; the greatest depth of thought appears unadorned and unpretentious. There are a few great men who can express the noblest sentiments without a wish that they should be heard, and who yet have no cause to dread listeners for the most trifling thing that they have uttered; and such is Beethoven in his Pianoforte Sonatas.

We frequently encounter the impression that Beethoven, in contradistinction to the other loftiest tone-poets, is specially the singer of melancholy and sorrow—of the most intense, passionate soul-suffering. Nothing can be less true. Certainly he depicted the night side of the human mind as no one had done before him. But when we view his compositions as a whole, there speaks to us out of them all—even the last, so deeply furrowed—a predominating vigorous cheerfulness, a sympathetic joy, a loving meditativeness, an earnest, resolute, fresh life. How often he sinks into blissful dreams, or gives himself up to childlike merriment! A mature man, yet seized at times by the extravagance of youth, while the battle of life makes him earnest, sometimes gloomy, but never faint-hearted or misanthropic (*weltschmerzlich*). "He was a *man*, take him for all in all;" we have not looked upon his like.

The special application of what has been said to the separate Sonatas would lead to nothing. Although it is indisputable that the emotions and frames of mind portrayed in them are almost infinite in compass, yet it would be proportionally difficult to express the same with regard to each single piece in words, the very definiteness of which would conclusively prove their inadequacy to the task. It is no empty phrase, however often it may have been repeated, that Music begins where Language ends,— of course with the proviso that the former content herself with the sovereignty in the domain assigned to her. How many tone-poems should we be compelled to characterize by words not only analogous to each other, but having the very same purport, even though a Goethe's wealth of language were at our command! and what a dissimilarity in the tone-forms would notwithstanding be apparent even to the most uninitiated listener!

Far more important than the invention of characteristic expressions is it, for those who would devote themselves to the study of Beethoven's pianoforte sonatas, to get a clear idea of them in *outline* as well as in *detail*. The comprehension of them is facilitated by this, with the natural result of a higher intellectual enjoyment. Is it not elevating to see how the most daring fancy, after having been nourished by deep thought, becomes the willing, submissive subject of the all-regulating mind? Beethoven never lost the reins, even in what seem the wildest flights of his genius: his Pegasus may spring up into highest space—he is able to direct and guide it.

No earnest, conscientious teacher should neglect to explain to those entrusted to him the essential nature of the laws which for centuries, by a kind of natural necessity, have developed themselves in the forms of instrumental music. They are so simple that their principal features may be made clear to the most childish comprehension, and every step in advance will bring with it a deeper insight. That Beethoven, in the closest relation to his great predecessors, submitted to these laws, makes his appearance doubly great: he did not come to destroy, but to fulfil the law.

O that our art, the most spiritual of all, were not bound by so many and such rigorous ties to matter! O that Beethoven's sonatas were within the reach of all educated minds, like the lyrics of our great poets! But not this alone does Nature deny to our art; she withholds from the greater number of those even who are striving as musicians and as pianists the full enjoyment of these lofty works, at least in their totality. They make demands upon the executants which are not easily met. Here and there we find the necessary talent. Were it but accompanied by the indispensable earnestness and diligence!

Beethoven's pianoforte music demands (apart from the

consideration of the extraordinarily difficult works) sound and solid execution. The first conditions of this are also the rarest, viz, a powerful and yet gentle touch, with the greatest possible independence of finger. Beethoven never writes difficulties merely to win laurels for those executants who shall overcome them, but neither is he deterred by any technical inconvenience, if it be necessary to give firm and clear expression to an idea. Thus we meet, in works reckoned amongst the easiest, with passages which presuppose a pretty high degree of technical skill; and since a pure style properly demands that there shall be at least the appearance of ease on the part of the performer,—with compositions of the intellectual depth of Beethoven's this is an indispensable qualification. Therefore it is not advisable to take or place the sonatas of our master in hands which are not educated for their reception. When that degree of progress has been attained which will insure the mastery of the technical difficulties, the enjoyment and advantage to be derived from their thorough study will be doubled, and the effort to grasp them intellectually unhindered.

The most essential figures which Beethoven employs are built upon the scale and the arpeggio. They belong, therefore, to that style which is specially designated the Clementi-Cramer school. The studies of these noble representatives of pure pianoforte playing will always be the best foundation for the performance of Beethoven's works, and the practice of them ought to accompany without intermission the study of the master. Happily, the rich productions of Beethoven's imagination offer fruits for every epoch of life and of— pianoforte-playing. We can reward the diligence of the studious child by allowing him to play the two sonatinas published after the master's death, which sound to us rather as if they had been written *for* than *by* a beginner. But we should carefully guard against giving to immature young minds pieces which, though easy in a technical point of view (and this, after all, is sometimes only *apparent*), require a power of conception and of performance far beyond the demands made upon the fingers. Who, for example, with any experience in musical life, does not remember having heard the Sonata Pathétique played with a *naïveté* of style which might prove the narrowness of the boundary line between the sublime and the ridiculous? And similar misconceptions are met with every day.

We give below a list of the sonatas in the order in which they ought to be studied, arranged with a view to the demands made upon the heart and mind, as well as upon the hand and finger of the performer. It is evident, however, that this cannot be done with mathematical precision, and that individual views and capability must, after all, decide; since *difficulty* and *ease* are but relative terms, and depend in each case upon other and pre-existing conditions. If, however, our attempt succeed so far as to render the selection easier to the student, and prevent his making any great mistakes, we shall not consider our trouble thrown away.

May Beethoven speedily find a home in every house—in every heart!

CLASSIFICATION OF BEETHOVEN'S PIANOFORTE SONATAS.

1. Op. 49, No. 2, in G major.
2. Op. 49, No. 1, in G minor.
3. Op. 14, No. 2, in G major.
4. Op. 14, No. 1, in E major.
5. Op. 79, in G major.
6. Op. 2, No. 1, in F minor.
7. Op. 10, No. 1, in C minor.
8. Op. 10, No. 2, in F major.
9. Op. 10, No. 3, in D major.
10. Op. 13, in C minor (*Pathétique*).
11. Op. 22, in B flat major.
12. Op. 28, in D major (*Pastorale*).
13. Op. 2, No. 2, in A major.
14. Op. 2, No. 3, in C major.
15. Op. 78, in F sharp major.
16. Op. 7, in E flat major.
17. Op. 26, in A flat major.
18. Op. 31, No. 3, in E flat major.
19. Op. 31, No. 1, in G major.
20. Op. 90, in E minor.
21. Op. 54, in F major.
22. Op. 27, No. 2, in C sharp minor (*Moonlight*).
23. Op. 31, No. 2, in D minor.
24. Op. 53, in C major.
25. Op. 27, No. 1, in E flat major.
26. Op. 81, in E flat major (*Les Adieux*).
27. Op. 57, in F minor (*Appassionata*).
28. Op. 110, in A flat major.
29. Op. 109, in E major.
30. Op. 101, in A major.
31. Op. 111, in C minor.
32. Op. 106, in B flat major (*The Giant*).

LIST OF BEETHOVEN'S WORKS.

Compiled from MARX *and* THAYER.

I.—COMPOSITIONS DESIGNATED AS *Opus*.

1. *Three Trios* for pianoforte, violin, and violoncello, in E flat, G major, and C minor; ded. to Prince Lichnowski; composed 1791-92.
2. *Three Sonatos* for piano, in F minor, A major, and C major; ded. to Joseph Haydn; pub. 1796.
3. *Trio* for violin, viola, and violoncello, in E flat; composed in Bonn before 1792.
4. *Quintet* for two violins, two violas, and violoncello, in E flat (from the octet for wind instruments, Op. 103); pub. 1795.
5. *Two Sonatas* for piano and violoncello, in F major and G minor; ded. to Frederic William II. of Prussia; composed in Berlin in 1796.
6. *Sonata* for piano, for four hands, in D major; pub. 1796-97.
7. *Sonata* for piano, in E flat; ded. to the Countess Babette von Keglevics; pub. 1797.
8. *Serenade* for violin, viola, and violoncello, in D major; pub. 1797.
9. *Three Trios* for violin, viola, and violoncello, in G major, D major, and C minor; ded. to the Count von Browne; pub. 1798.
10. *Three Sonatas* for piano, in C minor, F major, and D major; ded. to the Countess von Browne; pub. 1798.
11. *Trio* for piano, clarionet (or V.), and violoncello, in B flat; ded. to the Countess von Thun; pub. 1798.
12. *Three Sonatas* for piano and violin, in D major, A major, and E flat major; ded. to F. A. Salieri; pub. 1798-99.

13. *Sonata Pathétique* for piano, in C minor; ded. to Prince Lichnowski; pub. 1799.

14. *Two Sonatas* for piano, in E major and G major; ded. to the Baroness Braun; pub. 1799.

15. *First Concerto* for piano and orchestra, in C major; ded. to the Princess Odescalchi, *née* Countess von Keglevics; composed 1795.

16. *Quintet* for piano, clarionet, oboe, bassoon, and horn, in E flat major; ded. to the Prince von Schwarzenberg; performed 1798.

17. *Sonata* for piano and horn in F major; ded. to the Baroness Braun; composed 1800.

18. *Six Quartets* for two violins, viola, and violoncello, in F major, G major, D major, C minor, A major, and B flat major; ded. to Prince Lobkowitz; pub. 1800-1801.

19. *Second Concerto* for piano and orchestra, in B flat major; ded. to M. von Nickelsberg; composed 1798.

20. *Grand Septet* for violin, viola, violoncello, horn, clarionet, bassoon, and double-bass, in E flat; performed 1800.

21. *First Symphony* for orchestra, in C major; ded. to the Baron van Swieten; performed 1800.

22. *Grand Sonata* for piano, in B flat; ded. to the Count von Browne; composed 1800.

23. *Sonata* for piano and violin, in A minor; ded. to Count Moritz von Fries; pub. 1801.

24. *Sonata* for piano and violin, in F major; ded. to Count Moritz von Fries; pub. 1801 (originally together with Op. 23).

25. *Serenade* for flute, violin, and viola, in D major; pub. 1802.

26. *Sonata* for piano, in A flat; ded. to Prince Lichnowski; composed 1801.

27. *Two Sonatas*, quasi Fantasia, for piano, No. 1 in E flat major; ded. to the Princess Liechtenstein; No. 2 in C sharp minor; ded. to the Countess Julia Guicciardi; composed 1801 (?).

28. *Sonato* for piano, in D major; ded. to M. von Sonnenfels; composed 1801.

29. *Quintet* for two violins, two violas, and violoncello, in C major; ded. to Count von Fries; composed 1801.

30. *Three Sonatas* for piano and violin, in A major, C minor, and G major; ded. to the Emperor Alexander I. of Russia; composed 1802.
31. *Three Sonatas* for piano, in G major, D minor, and E flat major; composed 1802 (?).
32. "*To Hope,*" words from the "*Urania*" of Tiedge; pub. 1805 (first setting, *see* Op. 94).
33. *Bagatelles* for piano; composed 1782.
34. *Six Variations* for piano, in F major, on an original theme; ded. to the Princess Odescalchi; composed in 1802 (?).
35. *Fifteen Variations*, with a *Fugue;* for piano, on a theme from "*Prometheus,*" ded. to Count Moritz Lichnowski; composed 1802.
36. *Second Symphony* for orchestra, in D major; ded. to Prince Lichnowski; composed 1802.
37. *Third Concerto* for piano and orchestra, in C minor; ded. to Prince Louis Ferdinand of Prussia; composed 1800.
38. *Trio* for piano, clarionet (or V.), and violoncello (from the Septet, Op. 20); published 1805.
39. *Two Preludes* through all the major and minor keys, for piano or organ; composed 1789.
40. *Romance* for violin and orchestra, in G major; composed 1802 (?).
41. *Serenade* for piano and flute (or V.), in D major (from Op. 25); pub. 1803.
42. *Notturno* for piano and violoncello, in D major (from Op. 8); pub. 1804.
43. *Ballet:* "*The Men of Prometheus;*" composed 1800.
44. *Fourteen Variations* for piano, violin, and violoncello, on an original theme; composed 1802 (?).
45. *Three Marches* for piano, for four hands, in C major, E flat major, and D major; ded. to the Princess Esterhazy; composed 1802 (? 1801).
46. *Adelaïde:* words by Matthison; composed 1796.
47. *Sonata* for piano and violin, in A major; ded. to the violinist Rudolph Kreutzer; composed 1803.
48. *Six Spiritual Songs*, by Gellert; pub. 1803.

49. *Two Easy Sonatas* for piano, in G minor and G major; composed 1802 (?).

50. *Romance* for violin and orchestra, in F major; composed in 1802 (?).

51. *Two Rondos* for piano: No. 1 in C major; pub. 1798 (?); No. 2 in G major: ded. to the Countess Henriette von Lichnowski; pub. 1802.

52. *Eight Songs:* words by Claudius, Sophie von Mereau, Bürger, Goethe, and Lessing; partly composed in Bonn before 1792.

53. *Grand Sonata* for piano, in C major; ded. to Count Waldstein; composed in 1803 (?).

54. *Sonata* for piano, in F major; composed 1803 (?).

55. *Third Symphony* (Eroica) for orchestra, in E flat; ded. to Prince Lobkowitz; composed 1803-4.

56. *Triple Concerto* for piano, violin, and violoncello, with orchestra, in C major; composed 1804-5.

57. *Grand Sonata* for piano, in F minor; ded. to the Count von Brunswick; composed 1804.

58. *Fourth Concerto* for piano and orchestra, in G major; ded. to the Archduke Rudolph; composed 1806 (?).

59. *Three Quartets* for two violins, viola, and violoncello, in F major, E minor, and C major; ded. to Prince Rasoumowski; composed 1806.

60. *Fourth Symphony* for orchestra, in B flat; ded. to Count Oppersdorf; composed 1806.

61. *Concerto* for violin and orchestra, in D major; ded. to Stephan von Breuning; composed 1806.

62. *Overture:* "*Coriolanus*," in C minor; ded. to the dramatist Heinrich von Collin; composed 1807.

63. *Sonata* for piano, violin, and violoncello (from the Octet, Op. 103); pub. 1807.

64. *Sonata* for piano, violin, and violoncello (from the Trio, Op. 3); pub. 1807.

65. *Scena and Aria:* "*Ah, perfido!*" for soprano voice and orchestra; ded. to the Countess Clari; composed 1796.

66. *Twelve Variations* for piano and violoncello, in F major, on the theme, "*Ein Mädchen oder Weibchen,*" from Mozart's "*Zauberflöte;*" pub. 1798.

67. *Fifth Symphony* for orchestra, in C minor; ded. to Prince Lobkowitz and Count Rasoumowski; composed 1808 (?).

68. *Sixth Symphony* (*Pastorale*) for orchestra, in F major; ded. to Prince Lobkowitz and Count Rasoumowski; composed 1808 (?).

69. *Sonata* for piano and violoncello, in A major; ded. to Baron von Gleichenstein; pub. 1809.

70. *Two Trios* for piano, violin, and violoncello, in D major and E flat major; ded. to the Countess Marie Erdödy; composed 1808.

71. *Sextet* for two clarionets, two flutes, and two bassoons; performed 1804-5.

72. "*Fidelio.*" ("*Leonora*"), opera in two acts; composed 1804-5.

73. *Fifth Concerto* for piano and orchestra, in E flat; ded. to the Archduke Rudolph; composed 1809.

74. *Quartet* (tenth) for two violins, viola, and violoncello, in E flat; ded. to Prince Lobkowitz; composed 1809.

75. *Six Songs:* words by Goethe and Reissig; ded. to the Princess Kinsky; composed 1810.

76. *Variations* for piano, in D major, on an original (?) theme, afterwards employed as the "*Turkish March*" in the "*Ruins of Athens;*" ded. to his friend Oliva; pub. 1810.

77. *Fantasia* for piano, in G minor; ded. to the Count von Brunswick; composed 1809.

78. *Sonata* for piano, in F sharp major; ded. to the Countess von Brunswick; composed 1809.

79. *Sonatina* for piano, in G major; pub. 1810.

80. *Fantasia* for piano, orchestra, and chorus, in C minor; words—"*Schmeichelnd hold und lieblich klingen*"—by Kuffner; ded. to Joseph Maximilian, of Bavaria; performed 1808.

81a. *Sonata* for piano—"*Les Adieux,*"—in E flat; ded. to the Archduke Rudolph; composed 1809.

81b. *Sextet* for two violins, viola, violoncello, and two horns (*obbligato*), in E flat; pub. 1810.

82. *Four Ariettas* and a *Duet*, with pianoforte accompaniment; words of Nos. 2, 3, and 5 by Mestastasio; pub. 1811.

83. *Three Songs;* words by Goethe; ded. to the Princess Kinsky; composed 1810.

84. *Overture and incidental Music to* "*Egmont;*" composed 1809-10.

85. "*The Mount of Olives*," an oratorio; text by Franz Xaver Huber; composed 1800 (?).

86. *First Mass*, for four voices and orchestra, in C major; ded. to Prince Esterhazy; composed 1807.

87. *Trio* for wind instruments, in C major; performed 1797.

88. "*Das Glück der Freundschaft*," for voice and piano; pub. 1803.

89. *Polonaise* for piano, in C major; ded. to the Empress Elisabetha Alexiewna, of Russia; composed 1814.

90. *Sonata* for piano, in E minor; ded. to Count Moritz Lichnowski; composed 1814.

91. "*The Battle of Vittoria*," for orchestra; ded. to the Prince Regent of England; composed 1813.

92. *Seventh Symphony* for orchestra, in A major; ded. to Count Fries; composed 1812.

93. *Eighth Symphony* for orchestra, in F major; composed 1812.

94. "*To Hope;*" words from the "*Urania*" of Tiegde (second setting, *see* Op. 32).; composed 1816.

95. *Quartet* for two violins, viola, and violoncello, in F minor; ded. to Secretary Zmeskall; composed 1810.

96. *Sonata* for piano and violin, in G major; ded. to the Archduke Rudolph; composed 1810.

97. *Trio* for piano, violin, and violoncello, in B flat; ded. to the Archduke Rudolph; composed 1811.

98. "*An die ferne Geliebte*," a *Liederkreis;* words by Jeitteles; ded. to Prince Lobkowitz; composed 1816.

99. "*Der Mann von Wort*," for voice and piano; words by Kleinschmid; pub. 1815.

100. "*Merkenstein*," for one or two voices and piano; words by Rupprecht; composed 1814.

101. *Sonata* for piano, in A major; ded. to the Baroness Erdmann; composed 1815.

102. *Two Sonatas* for piano and violoncello, in C major and D major; ded. to the Countess Erdödy; composed 1815.

103. *Octet* for wind instruments, in E flat major; composed in Bonn before 1792.
104. *Quintet* for two violins, two violas, and violoncello, in C minor (from the Trio No. 3 of Op. 1); pub. 1819.
105. *Six Thèmes variés* for piano, with violin *ad libitum;* composed for George Thompson, 1818-19.
106. *Sonata* for piano, in B flat; ded. to the Archduke Rudolph; composed 1818.
107. *Ten Thèmes variés russes, écossais, tyroliens,* for piano, with violin *ad libitum;* composed for George Thompson, 1818-20.
108. *Twenty-five Scotch Melodies* for one or two voices and chorus (*obbligato*); pub. 1825.
109. *Sonata* for piano, in E major; ded. to Fräulein Brentano; composed 1821 (?).
110. *Sonata* for piano, in A flat major; composed 1821.
111. *Sonata* for piano, in C minor; ded. to the Archduke Rudolph; composed 1822.
112. "*Meeresstille und glückliche Fahrt,*" for four voices and orchestra; ded. to "the Author of the Poem, the immortal Goethe;" composed 1815.
113. *Overture:* "*The Ruins of Athens,*" composed 1811-12.
114. *Marches and Choruses* from "*The Ruins of Athens.*"
115. *Overture:* "*Namensfeier,*" in C major; ded. to Prince Radziwill; composed 1814.
116. *Terzetto* for soprano, tenor, and bass, with orchestral accompaniment; composed 1801.
117. *Overture and Choruses:* "*King Stephen;*" performed 1812.
118. *Elegy in memory of the Baroness Pasqualati:* "*Sanft wie du lebtest hast du vollendet;*" ded. to the Baron Pasqualati; composed 1814.
119. *Twelve Bagatelles* for piano; composed 1820-22.
120. *Thirty-three Variations* on a waltz by Diabelli; ded. to Madame Brentano; composed 1823.
121*a.* *Adagio, Variations, and Rondo,* for piano, violin, and violoncello, in G major; theme, "*Ich bin der Schneider Kakadu;*" pub. 1824.

121b. "*Opferlied*" for solo, chorus, and orchestra; words by Matthison; composed 1822.

122. "*In allen guten Stunden,*" for solo and chorus, with two clarionets, two horns, and two bassoons, words by Goethe; composed 1822.

123. *Missa Solemnis* for four voices, chorus, and orchestra, in D major; ded. to the Archduke Rudolph; composed 1818—1822.

124. *Overture:* "*Weihe des Hauses,*" in C major; ded. to Prince Galitzin; composed 1822.

125. *Ninth Symphony* (*Jupiter*), with final chorus on Schiller's "*Ode to Joy,*" for orchestra, four voices, and chorus, in D minor; ded. to Frederick William III. of Prussia; composed 1822-3.

126. *Six Bagatelles* for piano; composed about 1821.

127. *Quartet* for two violins, viola, and violoncello, in E flat; ded. to Prince Galitzin; composed 1824.

128. "*The Kiss;*" Arietta for voice and piano; composed 1822.

129. *Rondo capriccioso* in G major.

130. *Quartet* for two violins, viola, and violoncello, in B flat; ded. to Prince Galitzin; composed 1825.

131. *Quartet* for two violins, viola, and violoncello, in C sharp minor; ded. to the Baron von Stutterheim; composed 1826.

132. *Quartet* for two violins, viola, and violoncello, in A minor; ded. to Prince Galitzin; composed 1825.

133. *Grand Fugue* for two violins, viola, and violoncello, in B flat; ded. to the Cardinal Archduke Rudolph; composed 1825.

134. *Grand Fugue* (Op. 133 arranged for piano for four hands).

135. *Quartet* (the sixteenth) for two violins, viola, and 'cello, in F major; ded. to Herrn Wolfmeier; composed 1826.

136. "*Der Glorreiche Augenblick,*" cantata for four voices and orchestra; text by Dr. Weissenbach; ded. to Franz I., Emperor of Austria, Nicholas I., Emperor of Russia, and Frederick William III., King of Prussia; composed 1814.

137. *Fugue* for two violins, two violas, and 'cello, in D major; composed 1817.

138. *Ouverture caractéristique:* " *Leonora* " No. 1, in C major.

II. COMPOSITIONS DESIGNATED SIMPLY BY *Numbers*.

No. 1 *a*. *Twelve Variations* for piano and violin, in F major; Theme: " *Se vuol ballare,*" from Mozart's " *Figaro;*" ded. to Eleanore von Breuning; pub. 1793.

1 *b*. *Thirteen Variations* for piano, in A major; Theme: " *Es war einmal ein alter Mann;*" pub. 1794.

2. *Nine Variations* for piano, in A major; Theme: " *Quant è più bello;*" pub. 1797.

3 *a*. *Six Variations* for piano; Theme: " *Nel cor più non mi sento;*" composed 1795.

3 *b*. *Two Minuets* for piano, for four hands.

4. *Twelve Variations* for piano, in C major; Theme: " *Menuet à la Vigano;*" pub. 1796.

5 *a*. *Twelve Variations* for piano, in A major; Theme from the ballet of the " *Waldmädchen;*" pub. 1797.

5 *b*. *Twelve Variations* for piano and violoncello, in G major; Theme: " *See, the Conquering Hero comes!*" pub. 1804.

6. *Twelve Variations* for piano and violoncello, in F major. (*See* Op. 66.)

7. *Eight Variations* for piano in C major; Theme from Grétry's " *Richard Cœur de Lion;*" pub. 1798.

8. *Ten Variations* for piano in B flat major; Theme: " *La stessa, la stessissima;*" pub. 1799.

9. *Seven Variations* for piano, in F major; Theme: " *Kind willst du ruhig schlafen;*" pub. 1799.

10 *a*. *Eight Variations* for piano, in F major; Theme: " *Tändeln and Scherzen;*" composed 1799.

10 *b*. *Seven Variations* for piano and violoncello, in E flat; Theme from the " *Magic Flute;* " composed 1801 (?).

11. *Six very easy Variations* on an original Theme; composed 1801.

12. *Six easy Variations* for piano or harp, in F major; Theme : " *Air suisse;* " pub. 1799 (?).

13. *Twenty-four Variations* for piano, in D major, on a Theme by Righini; composed about 1790.

14—23. *Wanting.*
24. "*Der Wachtelschlag*," for voice and piano; words by Sauter; pub. 1804.
25. *Seven Variations* for piano, in C major; Theme: "*God save the King;*" pub. 1804.
26. *Five Variations* (favourite) for piano, in D major; Theme: "Rule, Britannia;" pub. 1804.
27. *Six Variations* for piano, for four hands, in D major, on an original Theme; composed 1800.
28. *Minuet* for piano.
29. *Prelude* for piano, in F minor; pub. 1805.
30, 31. *Wanting.*
32. "*To Hope*," by Tiedge (*see* Op. 94).
33, 34. *Wanting.*
35. *Andante* for piano in F major (originally in the Sonata, Op. 53), composed 1803 (?).
36. *Thirty-two Variations* for piano, in C minor, on an original Theme; pub. 1807.
37. *Wanting.*
38. "*Die Sehnsucht:*" four Melodies for voice and piano; text by Goethe; pub. 1810.

III. COMPOSITIONS DESIGNATED BY *Letters.*

A. INSTRUMENTAL MUSIC.

a. Trio for piano, violin, and violoncello (in one movement), in B flat; ded. to "my little friend, Maximiliana Brentano, for her encouragement in pianoforte playing;" composed 1812.
b. Rondo for piano and violin, in G major; pub. 1800.
c. Andante for piano, in G.
d. Sonata for piano, in C major (*incomplete*); composed 1796.
e. Two easy Sonatinas for piano, in G major and F major; composed in Bonn.
f. Three Sonatas for piano, in E flat major, F minor, and D major; ded. to the Elector Max. Friedrich; composed at the age of ten.
g. Rondo for piano, in A major; pub. 1784.

h. Andante on the text: "*Oh Hoffnung, du stählst die Herzen*" (Ex. for the Archduke Rudolph).

i. Favourite March of the Emperor Alexander.

k. Eight Variations for piano in B flat; Theme: "*Ich habe ein kleines Hüttchen nur.*"

l. Variations for piano, on a March by Dressler; composed at the age of ten.

m. Variations for piano, for four hands, on an original theme.

n. Variations for piano, for four hands, in A major.

o. Triumphal March for orchestra, in C major; performed 1813.

p. Second and Third Overtures to "*Leonora*" ("*Fidelio*"), in C major.

q. Overture to "*Fidelio*" ("*Leonora*" No. 4), in E flat.

r. Triumphal March for orchestra, in G major.

s. Three Duos for clarionet and bassoon, in C major, F major, and B flat; composed about 1800.

t. Minuet for piano (from the Septet, Op. 20).

u. Quintet (MS.), for two violins, two violas, and violoncello, in F major.

B. DANCE MUSIC.

Twelve Contre-danses.
Twelve Minuets for orchestra.
Six Minuets for piano.
Twelve *Danses Allemandes* for two violins and bass.
Seven Country Dances for piano.
Six Country Dances for piano.
Twelve *Ecossaises* for piano.
Six *Allemandes* for piano and violin.
Twelve Waltzes with Trios for orchestra.
Six Waltzes for two violins and bass.
Two Minuets for piano, for four hands.
Six Country Dances for piano.
Two Favourite Waltzes for piano, in B flat major and F minor.

C. VOCAL MUSIC.

a. Six Songs from Reissig's "*Blümchen der Einsamkeit:*"—

1. "*Sehnsucht,*" in E major.

2. "*Krieger's Abschied,*" in E flat.
   3. "*Der Jüngling in der Fremde,*" in B flat.
   4. "*An den fernen Geliebten,*" in G major.
   5. "*Der Zufriedene,*" in A major.
   6. "*Der Liebende,*" in D major.
 b. Three Songs:—
   1. "*An die Geliebte,*" in B flat.
   2. "*Das Geheimniss,*" in G major.
   3. "*So oder so! Nord oder Süd.*"
 c. Italian and German Songs:—
   1. "*La Partenza*" ("*ecco quel fiore*").
   2. "*Trinklied.*"
   3. "*Liedchen von der Ruhe.*"
   4. "*An die Hoffnung.*"
   5. "*Ich liebe dich, so wie du nich.*"
   6. "*Molly's Abschied.*"
   7. "*Ohne Liebe.*"
   8. "*Wachtelgesang.*"
   9. "*Marmotte.*"
  10. "*Maigesang.*"
  11. "*Feuerfarbe.*"
  12. "*Ecco quel fiori istanti.*"
 d. Songs, for one or more voices, from Shakspere, Byron, and Moore.
 e. "*Der Glorreiche Augenblick,*" for four voices and orchestra.
 f. "*Lied aus der Ferne.*"
 g. Three Songs from Tiedge.
 h. Three Songs.
 i. Three Songs.
 k. "*Oh! dass ich dir vom stillen Auge.*"
 l. "*Sehnsucht nach dem Rhein.*"
 m. "*Die Klage.*"
 n. Three Andantes.
 o. "*Ruf vom Berge.*"
 p. "*Der Bardengeist.*"
 q. "*Als die Geliebte sich trennen wollte.*"
 r. Elegy on the death of a Poodle.
 s. Arietta in A flat major.
 t. Canon in E flat major.

    u. "*Zärtliche Liebe.*"
    v. "*Resignation,*" "*Lisch' aus,*" in E major.
    w. Canon for six voices.
    x. Canon for four voices.
    y. Canon for three voices.
    z. Canon written in the album of Director Neide.
    tz. Song of the Monks, from Schiller's "*Wilhelm Tell.*"
    a^2. "*Song of the Nightingale.*"
    b^2. "*Germania's Wiedergeburt,*" for four voices and orchestra.
    c^2. "*Abschiedsgesang an Wien's Bürger.*"
    e^2. Final songs from (1) "*Die Ehrenpforte,*" in D major; (2) "*Die gute Nachricht.*"
    f^2. "*Andenken von Matthison*"—allegretto.
    g. Three-part *Song.*

IV. COMPOSITIONS WHICH APPEARED AFTER BEETHOVEN'S DEATH, WITHOUT BEING DESIGNATED AS *Op.* OR *No.*

    a. "*Beethoven's Heimgang,*" for voice and piano.
    b. "*An Sie,*" Song, in A flat major.
    c. Two Songs:—
        1. "*Seufzer eines Ungeliebten.*"
        2. "*Die laute Klage.*"
    d. "*Die Ehre Gottes in der Natur,*" for four voices and orchestra, in C major.
    e. Cantata: "*Europa steht.*"
    f. Song, "*Gedenke mein.*"
    g. Empfindungen bei Lydia's Untreu," in E flat.
    h. "*Equali,*" two pieces for four trombones.
    i. Allegretto for orchestra.
    k. Three Quartets.
    l. Rondo for piano and orchestra.
    m. Octet for wind instruments.
    n. Rondino for eight-part harmony.
    o. Two Trios for piano, violin, and 'cello.
    p. Military March for piano.
    q. "*Lament at Beethoven's Grave.*"
    r. "*The Last Musical Thought.*"

www.ingramcontent.com/pod-product-compliance
Lightning Source LLC
Chambersburg PA
CBHW020912230426
43666CB00008B/1422